W9-DJE-950

Columbia College Library
600 South Michigan
Chicago, IL 60605

COMMONWEALTH
SECRETARIAT

CHECK

IN POCKET

the Commonwealth:

941 P228c

a Family of Nations

WITHDRAWN

Liz Paren
Caroline Coxon
Cheryl Dorall

ENTERED OCT 2 8 2004

Published by:
Commonwealth Secretariat
Marlborough House
Pall Mall, London SW1Y 5HX, United Kingdom

© Commonwealth Secretariat, 2003

All rights reserved. No part of this publication may
be reproduced, stored in a retrieval system, or transmitted in
any form or by any means, electronic or mechanical, including
photocopying, recording or otherwise without the permission
of the publisher.

Further copies may be purchased from:
Publications Unit
Commonwealth Secretariat
Telephone: +44 (0)20 7747 6342
Facsimile: +44 (0)20 7839 9081
Email: r.jones-parry@commonwealth.int
Website: http//www.thecommonwealth.org

ISBN: 0-85092-753-6
Price: £8.95

Designed by Julie Nelson Rhodes
Printed by SRM Production Services Sdn. Bhd. Malaysia

Wherever possible, the Commonwealth Secretariat uses paper
sourced from sustainable forests or from sources that minimise
a destructive impact on the environment.

contents

'I know about the Commonwealth Games – they're exciting'

'The Commonwealth is not for ordinary people – it's for politicians'

'Does the Commonwealth take any notice of young people?'

'Does the Commonwealth matter in the world today?'

chapter 1
what is the Commonwealth?

How much do you know about the Commonwealth?

Not a lot?

You are not alone. There are many people living in Commonwealth countries who know very little about this 54-member grouping of countries. They enthusiastically support their sportsmen and women in the four-yearly Commonwealth Games; they may read the headlines which accompany the two-yearly Commonwealth Heads of Government Meetings (CHOGMs).

But that might be all they know.

This book has been written to fill this gap, to tell you about the Commonwealth; about how it came into being and developed into the association it is today; about why it matters; about what it does for ordinary people; and especially about its relationship with young people.

The Commonwealth matters because it stands for principles and values which are of great importance in our troubled world:
- democracy
- respect for human rights
- the rule of law
- peace
- justice
- co-operation
- sustainable development

You may think these are just high-sounding words that have little connection with your daily life. What have they got to do with going to school, passing exams, looking for work, getting on with your family, trying to make a living, struggling against poverty and disease? It is a firm belief of the Commonwealth that people need to be given choices and opportunities if they are to be able to improve their lives. Those choices can only occur if ordinary people are involved in making decisions and if everyone's views are respected. The Commonwealth is not just about governments – it is essentially about people working together.

'It is not for governments … alone. It is for all the people of the Commonwealth.'

'a powerful force for co-operation in the promotion of peace, prosperity and equity'

> **Did you know**
> that all the top cricket teams come from Commonwealth countries?

> **Did you know**
> that nearly one-third of the world's population lives in Commonwealth countries?

> **Did you know**
> that 11 of the world's top rugby teams are from Commonwealth countries?

> **Did you know**
> that half of the people in the Commonwealth are under 25?

Young people and the Commonwealth

On the second Monday in March people throughout the Commonwealth celebrate Commonwealth Day. The day is chosen because children all over the Commonwealth are at school then. In many Commonwealth countries young people in and out of school take part in parades, musical performances, competitions, sports contests, debates, fashion shows, food tastings, dance events and other forms of celebration. In the classroom they research the cultures of other countries, write essays, and take part in debates.

Each year a different theme is chosen for Commonwealth Day. That of 2003 was 'Partners in Development'; the theme for 2004 is 'Building a Commonwealth of Freedom'. The Queen, as Head of the Commonwealth, sends a message to all Commonwealth countries based on that theme. In many countries special observances take place in which people of all religions come together to pray, to affirm their belief in the ideals of the Commonwealth and to celebrate. The largest of these takes place in Westminster Abbey in London, which Queen Elizabeth attends.

'a multicultural, multi-ethnic ... force for good'

'Commonwealth Day is about celebrating the common values that bind our countries and our people together. Because of the Commonwealth, school children in Tanzania and, for example, in Australia, are not complete strangers. They speak the same language, they experience similar school systems, they share similar values, and, in many respects, they share the same world view.' (Don McKinnon, Commonwealth Secretary-General)

A Zulu dancer taking part in a Commonwealth Day Observance in Westminster Abbey

The Commonwealth recognises that its future lies
with the young people of the Commonwealth.
You are that future – it is your Commonwealth.

'a unique family of nations'

There are many ways in which you could be involved – maybe this book will
encourage you to find out more. There is a list of useful addresses and
websites at the end of the book.

chapter 2
the Commonwealth Games

Every four years, the 54 countries of the Commonwealth, large and small, rich and poor, gather together to celebrate their friendship through sport at the Commonwealth Games.

When the Games started in 1930, the original constitution said that although they would be designed on the Olympic model, 'they should be merrier and less stern'. Helped by a common language and because the desire to win seems to co-exist with a real spirit of unity and friendship, the Commonwealth Games are known as the **'Friendly Games'**.

The vision of the Commonwealth Games Federation is 'to promote a unique, friendly, world-class Games, and to develop sport for the benefit of the people, the nations and the territories of the Commonwealth and thereby strengthen the Commonwealth.' In achieving this aim, the Games also demonstrate some of the values held by all Commonwealth nations.

Then and now

The first Commonwealth Games, known then as the British Empire Games, were held in Hamilton, Canada, in 1930. Accommodation

was in a school, where competitors slept 24 to a classroom! Four hundred athletes from just 11 countries took part and women only competed in swimming. Since then, the Games have been held every four years, with a gap in 1942 and 1946 because of the Second World War.

1954 In Vancouver, Roger Bannister (above) of England and Australian John Landy ran the first sub-four minute miles in a race. The event was the first to be televised live across the globe.

1958 The Cardiff Games were South Africa's last until their post-apartheid return in 1994. Their team had been selected on the basis of race and colour rather than ability, which raised many objections from other nations.

1982 In Brisbane, in the men's 200 metres final, Allan Wells from Scotland and Mike McFarlane from England shared the gold medal (right). Judges were unable to separate the pair at the winning post.

1970 In Edinburgh, metric distances were adopted and electronic photo finish technology was used for the first time. Her Majesty Queen Elizabeth II attended in her capacity as Head of the Commonwealth.

1986 Known as the 'Boycott Games' and held in Edinburgh, 32 Commonwealth nations chose not to attend to show their opposition to apartheid in sport.

1998 For the first time in its history the Commonwealth Games were held in Asia, in Kuala Lumpur. These were also the first Games at which there were team sports as well as individual events.

The Games of 2002

In 2002, the English city of Manchester hosted the Games. More than 4,000 athletes from 72 nations and territories participated. For the first time in a major international sports competition, events for disabled athletes were held alongside those for able-bodied athletes, and their medals were included in the overall total.

The Games were the centrepiece of a six-month long programme of events called the Spirit of Friendship Festival, in which young and old celebrated the cultural diversity of Commonwealth nations with many arts events, and marked the Queen's Golden Jubilee and her 50 years as Head of the Commonwealth.

On Commonwealth Day, 11 March 2002, a special Jubilee baton was sent on its way from Buckingham Palace. It held Her Majesty's Commonwealth Message and was carried by up to 5,000 people in relay, on its journey across countries, through towns and villages across the Commonwealth, to be returned to Manchester

on 25 July. The message was read out by the Queen at the opening ceremony of the Games.

Many new facilities were built for the Games, promising to benefit the people of Manchester in the future. Not only will there be a lasting sporting legacy, but also regeneration of parts of the city that had fallen into a bad state of repair, and a significant investment in health, educational, social and business programmes.

Going for gold!

Watching the Commonwealth Games on TV, it's easy to be swept away by the sporting successes of famous athletes in high profile sports. We may forget that a few moments of glory on the winners' podium have been preceded by years of training and struggle and very often, financial hardship. This is even more the case for those competing in less popular sports, without profitable sponsorship deals to help them with their expenses. See pages 13-16 for some profiles of Commonwealth athletes.

Of the 54 countries that make up the Commonwealth, 32 of these are small states. One of the great things about the Commonwealth is the fact that it gives each country, no matter how small, an equal voice and the same opportunities to participate.

In the early days of the Games, most of the competitors were men, and few events allowed for women to take part. In Manchester 2002, there were equal numbers of male and female athletes, and women competed across all sports except rugby 7s. This reflects the strong commitment to gender equality across the Commonwealth, shown in the Indian women's hockey team (see page 15).

we stick together

At 17, **Ryan Bester** became the youngest lawn bowler to ever compete for Canada, at the Commonwealth Games in Manchester 2002. He had already been bowling for eight years by then! A lot of people see bowls as a sport for older people, but, in fact, it requires a great deal of physical and mental stamina. It is wonderful to find an international event that gives an opportunity to excel without involving speed and strength. The Commonwealth Games have something for everyone!

'The Commonwealth Games were my first international event. I, for one, found everyone to be friendly and just by walking through the village everyone says hi and talks. It was very nice to see and be part of it.'

'After competing I did think differently about the Commonwealth. I see that we are one strong unit that sticks together.'

'I did see a lot of unity and non-discrimination. Just by going on the bus to the venue it didn't matter what colour or religion, everyone met and treated each other equally. I did not see one act of prejudice or discrimination towards anyone. Also everyone played fairly. I myself did not see one person cheating to gain for themselves.'

Did you know

Although there are 54 Commonwealth countries, there are 72 Commonwealth Games Associations (CGAs) that can enter a team in the Commonwealth Games.

For example, the United Kingdom is a single Commonwealth country, but has seven CGAs. Scotland, England, Northern Ireland, Wales, Isle of Man, Jersey, and Guernsey all compete in the Games as separate nations.

a real boost

Ofisa Ofisa is from Samoa, a group of small islands in the Pacific. He's 26 years old, and an IT consultant as well as being a successful weightlifter for his country, winning a silver and a bronze medal at the Manchester Commonwealth Games. He had a wonderful time and this is what he said about it.

'Samoa always looks forward to participating in the Commonwealth Games and it is a major sporting highlight for our country every four years. I guess because we have such close ties and merging histories we have a feeling of belonging to the Commonwealth Games.

It has a special feel about it. Although it is dubbed the Friendly Games it does not deter from the fact that it is a prestigious international multi-sport competition and each athlete is determined to do their best and compete to their best but there certainly was a feeling of friendliness in the Manchester Games Village.

The weather unfortunately was not great but the people of Manchester made our stay very warm and welcoming. From hopping onto the buses to take us to the Games to the fantastic food in the Village dining room, I have to say Manchester 2002 was a real buzz and I felt at home with the other athletes from 72 nations. I was really pleased to see elite athletes with a disability take part because this showed the Games included everyone.

I am grateful to our Lord for giving me the strength to execute my goal of winning at Manchester, so this is a very important milestone in my life and one which I feel very fortunate to have achieved. I'm so glad I have been able to repay my parents and my wife for their faith in my ability to achieve. I am also grateful to my mentor, Aitkin Fruean, who was a great source of strength to me in the lonely process of training and dreaming the dream to win a Commonwealth Games medal.

It is a real honour to represent Samoa and my family and so I was very pleased to win medals as it means a great deal to a small nation, but definitely the support from Samoa is a real boost and has a real positive spin off.'

The Commonwealth Games are the most visible demonstration of all the things that are good about the Commonwealth as a family of nations. The sportsmen and women who compete are not only great ambassadors for their own countries, but, as individuals, show the world a way of relating to other human beings that the Commonwealth sincerely values and seeks to emulate.

'Today, it is time to admire the new face of Indian hockey — gutsy women with fire in their bellies. It is time to celebrate the story of a team comprising girls from rural, tribal areas; girls who have toiled for years on dusty grounds in small town schools — in Aarkhand, Haryana and Punjab; girls who are forced to support their families at a young age but never give up; girls whose voices have been muffled for demanding more respect from officials; girls who value the national jersey and play the game hard.'
Hindustan Times

truly friendly

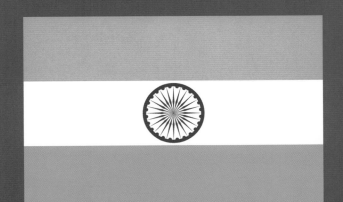

Mamta Kharab is one such girl, who became a star overnight after her golden goal in the final against England

'To represent their country is the dream of every sportsman and woman and among them, only some get the chance. I feel very happy that I make my country proud. I feel so proud but the effort was not only mine. It was the effort of our whole team.'

'There were top teams in the tournament, from wealthy countries. In spite of this we won and achieved glory for my country. I played like a woman possessed!'

Mamta's winning goal proved to be controversial. She scored from a penalty corner just as the half-time hooter sounded in extra time. It was first disallowed, then the umpire changed her mind and the English team lodged an appeal.

However, in the spirit of the Friendly Games and for the good of hockey, England decided not to proceed with a second appeal, saying: 'the entire England team wish to congratulate India on the game'.

Truly the 'Friendly Games'!

like everyone else

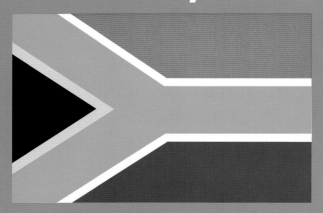

In 1998, 15-year-old **Natalie du Toit** competed for South Africa at the Kuala Lumpur Games. In February 2001, travelling to school, she was involved in a horrific accident, which resulted in her losing part of her leg. She remembered everything at the time of the crash and that the sight of her leg was 'like it is when you drop a tomato from a great height'. With remarkable courage and determination, she returned to her training after only three months admitting it was 'excruciatingly painful', yet she is still living up to her early potential, winning two gold medals at Manchester 2002, in disabled swimming events and, perhaps even more impressively, reaching the final of the able-bodied 800 metre final. She was voted top athlete of the Commonwealth Games.

'There is definitely a different spirit at the Commonwealth Games. Well, on my arrival in Manchester, I was warmly welcomed by the public. The people never looked at my leg to tell who I was; they were actually recognising my face and it made me feel like I was part of society again, that I was one of the norm and like everyone else. The public treated the disabled swimmers with utmost acceptance, which was fantastic, as it was the first time I was competing as a disabled swimmer. The stands were always full and the crowds were always cheering and encouraging the swimmers.

My achievements are goals which I set when I was younger and worked really hard to achieve. I hope I have brought back to my nation that many disabled people would like to be seen as normal people who with hard work and determination can achieve anything. I lost part of my leg but I am like anyone else. I have not changed since my accident. With the grace of the Lord I hope that I will be able to realise my ultimate goal – the 2004 Olympics. If I can touch just one person and make them think differently about themselves and what they are striving for then I am truly happy.

I feel extremely honoured to represent my country. My country has stood by me, and my swimming family, especially my coach. This I truly appreciate and would like to thank them from the bottom of my heart.'

chapter 3
countries of the Commonwealth

There are 54 countries in the Commonwealth.

Thirty-two of these member countries are small states in most of which the population numbers less than 1.5 million people. There are more than 1.7 billion people in the Commonwealth.

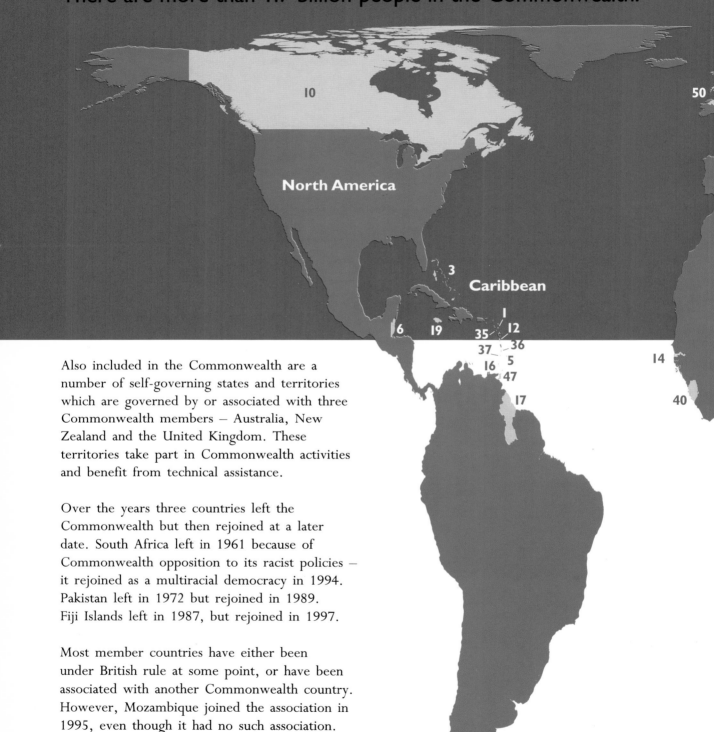

Also included in the Commonwealth are a number of self-governing states and territories which are governed by or associated with three Commonwealth members – Australia, New Zealand and the United Kingdom. These territories take part in Commonwealth activities and benefit from technical assistance.

Over the years three countries left the Commonwealth but then rejoined at a later date. South Africa left in 1961 because of Commonwealth opposition to its racist policies – it rejoined as a multiracial democracy in 1994. Pakistan left in 1972 but rejoined in 1989. Fiji Islands left in 1987, but rejoined in 1997.

Most member countries have either been under British rule at some point, or have been associated with another Commonwealth country. However, Mozambique joined the association in 1995, even though it had no such association.

Countries hoping to become members must have some past or present association with a member, must practise democracy and have to be accepted by all members.

For a key to the numbers shown here, and to see the flags of the Commonwealth nations, turn to page 20.

For the story of how the Commonwealth came into being, see Chapters 5 and 6.

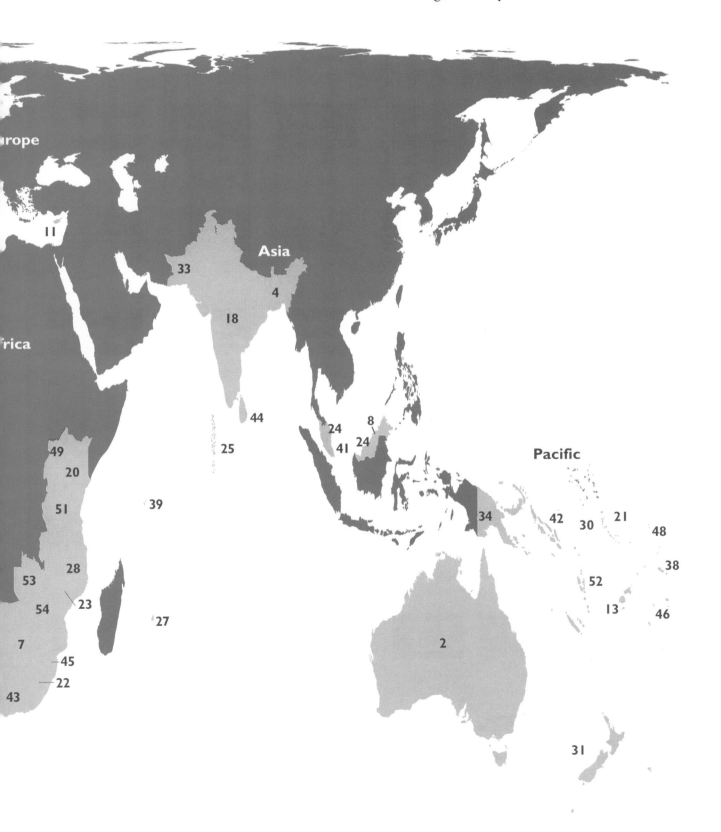

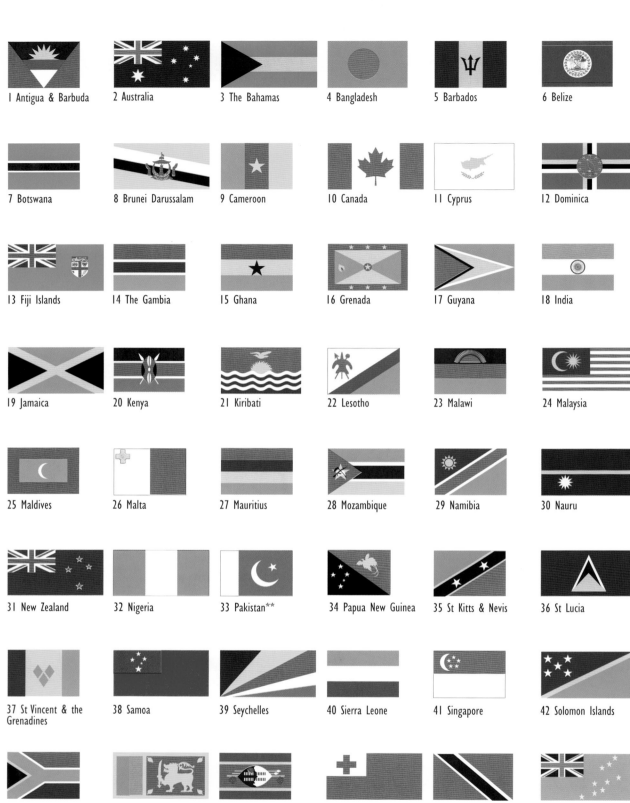

1 Antigua & Barbuda

2 Australia

3 The Bahamas

4 Bangladesh

5 Barbados

6 Belize

7 Botswana

8 Brunei Darussalam

9 Cameroon

10 Canada

11 Cyprus

12 Dominica

13 Fiji Islands

14 The Gambia

15 Ghana

16 Grenada

17 Guyana

18 India

19 Jamaica

20 Kenya

21 Kiribati

22 Lesotho

23 Malawi

24 Malaysia

25 Maldives

26 Malta

27 Mauritius

28 Mozambique

29 Namibia

30 Nauru

31 New Zealand

32 Nigeria

33 Pakistan**

34 Papua New Guinea

35 St Kitts & Nevis

36 St Lucia

37 St Vincent & the Grenadines

38 Samoa

39 Seychelles

40 Sierra Leone

41 Singapore

42 Solomon Islands

43 South Africa

44 Sri Lanka

45 Swaziland

46 Tonga

47 Trinidad & Tobago

48 Tuvalu

49 Uganda

50 United Kingdom

51 United Republic of Tanzania

52 Vanuatu

53 Zambia

54 Zimbabwe**

** These two countries have been suspended from the Councils of the Commonwealth: Pakistan in October 1999 and Zimbabwe in March 2002.

The flags illustrated are stylised representations and neither the proportions nor the colours are guaranteed true.

chapter 4

diversity in the Commonwealth

Geographical diversity Among the 54 members of the Commonwealth there are marked geographical contrasts. The organisation contains the second largest country in the world (in terms of area), the second most highly populated, and many of the world's smallest nations. It includes a nation where there are over 6,000 people for every square kilometre, and several where there are fewer than 5 people for the same area. It includes some of the most urbanised societies in the world, where there are cities in which over a million people live, and countries where less than 20% of the people live in towns. It includes a handful of highly developed nations and many developing ones. Read on for some facts and figures about a selection of Commonwealth countries.

A small, densely populated country: Singapore

Singapore has an area of less than 1,000 square kilometres. It is densely populated and highly urbanised and is the most highly developed nation in the Commonwealth.

Capital Singapore
Population 4 million
Area 647.5 sq km
Population density 6,205 per sq km
Percentage of people living in towns 100%

Singapore is a string of islands in south-east Asia, just north of the Equator. The land in Singapore is flat, much of it having been reclaimed from swamps — the highest point is only 166 metres. There is hardly any arable land so almost everyone lives in the city. Singapore has a highly developed economy, with manufacturing industries making electronics and chemicals for export, and a range of services. It has the biggest harbour in the world — it is also one of the busiest. The climate is hot and humid, with frequent thunderstorms.

MALAYSIA

Johor Strait

Lim Chu Kang
Sembawang
Pulau Ubin
Pulau Tekong
Serangoon
SINGAPORE
Jurong
Changi
City
Katong
Queenstown
Jurong Island
Sentosa
Strait of Singapore
Pulau Sudong
Pulau Senang

Singapore's world class container port

A large, sparsely populated country: Canada

Canada is the largest country in the Commonwealth in terms of area. Yet it is sparsely populated, with a population density of fewer than five people per square kilometre.

Did you know that CANADA has the longest coastline in the world?

Canada is the second largest country in the world. It has almost a quarter of the world's supply of fresh water in its thousands of lakes and rivers. Plains cover most of Canada, but there are mountains in the west, and lowlands in the south-east. The highest point is Mount Logan (5,959 metres). Over 50% of the land area of Canada is occupied by forests. Much of the country has very cold weather and is often snowbound, but summers in the prairies can be very hot. Some areas of Canada are very dry, with less than 350 mm of rainfall a year. In the western province of British Columbia, however, the rainfall exceeds 1,000 mm a year. Canada has rich natural resources including a number of minerals and energy sources,

Capital Ottawa
Population 31 million
Area 9,215,430 sq km
Population density 3.3 per sq km
Percentage of people living in cities 77%

as well as timber and fish. It is a highly developed industrialised society. Most of its people live within 350 kilometres of the southern border with the USA.

A large, densely populated country: India

India is the second most highly populated country in the world. It contains several towns in which live over three million people.

Did you know that well over half of the people of the Commonwealth live in India?

Capital New Delhi
Population 1,015,923,000
Area 3,287,263 sq km
Population density 309 per sq km
Percentage of people living in towns 28%

A huge country in southern Asia, India has four distinct regions. To the north is the mountainous area of the

Himalayas; to the north-west lies desert. Much of the centre of the country is made up of the plain of the mighty River Ganges and its tributaries. This is the most fertile area of the country – and is consequently densely populated. To the south is the Deccan tableland. Its highest point is Kanchenjunga (8,598 metres). India is rich in natural resources, having the fourth largest coal reserves in the world. Most of the land area is used for farming. Although India has several huge cities, and is highly industrialised, 70% of its people still live in the rural areas. One of India's most successful industries is the export of computer software. The climate varies greatly across the country, but severe weather conditions can be a problem, with flooding and earthquakes common occurrences.

New Dehli

A small country: Seychelles

Fifteen of the member countries of the Commonwealth have land areas of less than 1,000 square kilometres. Nine of these have fewer than 100,000 people. All of these are islands. One of the main achievements of the Commonwealth has been the work that it has done to assist its smaller members. And, it should be remembered that in the Commonwealth, the smallest member is accorded exactly the same rights as the largest.

Capital Victoria
Population 81,000
Area 455 sq km
Population density 178 per sq km
Percentage of people living in towns 62%

A popular tourist destination, this archipelago of over 100 islands lies in the western part of the Indian Ocean. Most of the islands are made of coral and are low-lying. The three main ones (on which most of the people live) are made of

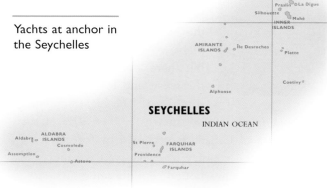

Yachts at anchor in the Seychelles

granite and have central ridges of mountains. The highest point is Morne Seychellois (905 metres). Tourism is an important industry in Seychelles, and it employs about 30% of the labour force. Tuna fishing is also being developed. Seychelles has a tropical climate, meaning that it is hot and humid, with a high rainfall.

A sparsely populated country: Botswana

As well as Canada, there are several other countries in the Commonwealth that are very sparsely populated.

Capital Gaborone
Population 1,597,000
Area 582,000 sq km
Population density 2.7 per sq km
Percentage of people living in towns 50%

Botswana is a landlocked country in Southern Africa. Most of the country consists of the Kalahari Desert, a vast tableland. The highest point is the Tsodilo Hills (1,489 metres). A number of valuable minerals are mined in the desert areas of Botswana, especially diamonds. 80% of the people make a living from subsistence agriculture, some from growing crops, but mostly from raising animals. Botswana has a temperate climate, receiving its rainfall in the summer months of October to April. The winter is dry, and then the nights

can be cold, even frosty. Most people live in the south-east of the country.

Mochudi – a traditional town

A multitude of languages

In most Commonwealth countries, English is used for official business or is widely spoken and understood. It is taught in primary schools and is often the language of secondary and tertiary education. The sharing of a common language is important for the Commonwealth. When Commonwealth leaders, politicians and civil servants meet they can communicate easily with each other. There is no need for the translators and headphones that are necessary for most international meetings.

A brief look at the other languages which the people of the Commonwealth speak tells us more about its amazing diversity. There are a small number of countries, for example, where English is not used as an official language at all. Mozambique, which became a member of the Commonwealth in 1995, uses Portuguese as its official language, reflecting the fact that it was a Portuguese colony.

In over a dozen countries English is a joint official language. Sometimes the other official language is far more widely spoken than English – for example, French in Cameroon, Hindi in India, and Kiswahili in Tanzania. In some cases the second official language is that of a minority group – for example Maori in New Zealand, French in Canada, and Welsh in Wales (part of the United Kingdom). Sometimes countries have decided to adopt several official languages, to give different ethnic groups an equal voice. Singapore, for example, has Chinese, Malay and Tamil as official languages as well as English; South Africa has adopted English, Afrikaans and nine African languages all as official languages.

In most Commonwealth countries there are other languages which are widely spoken. Sometimes there is just one such language, for example Setswana in Botswana; often there are several, for example Ghana has eight national languages, Zambia has seven main languages, India has 17 regional languages, Pakistan has four. In a handful of cases, there are hundreds of different languages and dialects spoken in a country. Nigeria, for example, has three main languages (Hausa, Yoruba and Igbo) but over 200 others; the people of Papua New Guinea speak over 700 different languages; those of Solomon Islands speak 80; and in tiny Vanuatu over 100 different languages and dialects are spoken.

A diversity of religious beliefs Within the countries of the Commonwealth can be found followers of all the world's main religions – Christians, Muslims, Hindus, Buddhists, Sikhs and Jews.

Hinduism in India

Over 80% of the people of India are Hindus. Hinduism revolves around the family, with each home having its shrine to a chosen god (left). Several times a day incense, flowers and prayers are offered to the image of the chosen god. At temples, the priest looks after the god's image there – believers come to bring gifts and to pray. At the larger temples groups of believers gather to pray, sing hymns and to join in rituals.

Sikhism in the United Kingdom

There are about 20 million Sikhs in the world today. The biggest Sikh community outside the Punjab is in the United Kingdom, where they number about 400,000.

The focus of worship is the gurdwara. There are about 100 gurdwaras in the UK. Outside each flies the yellow, triangular, Sikh flag. Inside is kept the holy book of Sikhism, the Guru Granth Sahib. This symbolises the presence of God. Services in the United Kingdom usually take place on Sundays. Every service concludes with a communal, vegetarian meal.

A Sikh gurdwara in the UK

Buddhism in Sri Lanka

It was in Sri Lanka that the teachings of Buddha were first written down, forming the Pali Canon. Today about 70% of the population of Sri Lanka are Buddhist.

In Sri Lanka there is a famous Buddhist festival. This is the Festival of the Sacred Tooth which takes place in the city of Kandy in August. A sacred tooth, believed to have belonged to Buddha, is paraded through the streets on the back of an elephant. The people make much noise on drums, by blowing conch shells and chanting. There are also fire-eaters, dancers and drummers.

Muslims at prayer

Islam in Malaysia

Over half the people of Malaysia are Muslim, most of them Malays. Islam was established in the peninsular in the 15th century. However, there is a long tradition of tolerance in the country, since there are also many Chinese people (many of whom are Buddhists), and Indian people (who are mostly Hindus). There are also significant Sikh and Christian communities.

Followers of the different faiths all enjoy the religious festivals which fill the Malaysian calendar. For the Muslims the most important is Hari Raya Puasa (Eid al-Fitr) which takes place at the end of the fasting month of Ramadan. For three days there is great rejoicing.

Procession in Malta (below)

Christianity in Malta

The people of Malta are mostly Roman Catholic. They mark Good Friday, the day when Jesus Christ was crucified, with solemn processions in which men wearing white robes carry statues through the streets. The young people and children dress up as characters from the Bible. In the villages and towns of the islands, the summer months are marked by a succession of feast days. On these the Catholics celebrate the birthday of chosen saints, or Mary, the mother of Jesus. The churches are full of flowers; outside, bells are rung and fireworks let off, as the Maltese people enjoy the special foods of the feast.

Christianity in Africa

Many countries in the Commonwealth are mostly Christian, but it is in Africa that this world religion is spreading most rapidly. There are probably some 140 million African Christians.

Most parts of Africa had their first contacts with European Christian missionaries in the 1900s: today they have made the religion their own. Black church leaders bring aspects of African culture into their worship – such as healing, song and dance. There are about 10,000 new churches and religious movements in Africa – probably 15% of African Christians belong to one of them.

Christians worshipping in Ghana

Cultural contrasts What makes up a people's culture? It is their way of life and their customs; it is the music they like to play, the food they eat, the art they make; it is their language and their religion.

Families and the way they live

The family is the fundamental social unit for all humanity. It is in the family that children grow and learn about their culture. In many parts of the Commonwealth, the number of people that live together in one family unit is small – one or two parents, and their children (often referred to as a nuclear family). Such families are common wherever people live in towns. But there are many countries in the Commonwealth where most people live on the land – and here it is more usual to find larger families living together (an extended family). All the family members can then work together to grow the crops and look after the animals on which the family depends.

On the following pages you are invited to look at family life in a selection of Commonwealth countries. There is a deliberate emphasis on families who live in rural areas because it is here that people are most affected by custom and tradition. You should remember that in all these countries many families live in cities – but in the cities the old traditions and customs have less impact on people's lives.

Living in a flat in Singapore

In Singapore most families are nuclear and live in high rise blocks of flats – a common way of living where space is in short supply. People in the flats have electricity and running water.

Sometimes there may be a swimming pool near the flats. Women put their washing onto long poles outside the windows of the flats. They buy their food in the markets – very little of the food there is grown in Singapore. There is not enough space to build schools for everyone, so double shifts at primary schools are common.

A time of celebration is the Mooncake Festival. This takes place when the Moon is full in September or October. The children love to eat moon cakes – these are round with pastry on the outside and tasty fillings, such as red bean paste. Puppet shows tell old Chinese stories, and the shops are full of coloured lanterns in the shapes of fish, birds and aeroplanes.

Living on the shamba in Kenya

The capital of Kenya, Nairobi, is a large and sophisticated city, in which over two million people live. However, most people rely on the land to make their living. In the Kikuyu country, each family has a smallholding or shamba of between 2 and 8 hectares. They grow maize and beans to eat, as well as many different kinds of fruit and vegetables. They keep some domestic animals, such as chickens, sheep, goats and maybe a cow or two. They also grow coffee, which they sell in exchange for cash. Many trees provide shade, and are useful for firewood and building.

It is very unusual to have electricity, so most women cook using firewood or charcoal. Few families have running water, so water has to be fetched. Most families have a radio. Home for the family consists of several buildings – the house where people sleep, stores, the kitchen, the bathroom and toilet. Most of the family life takes place out of doors because it is usually warm. The family has to get up at dawn.

Children start their walk to school before 7, neatly dressed in their uniforms. It is their responsibility to keep the school clean, and to keep the garden neat. They help with the work at home too.

The women walk to market in the village, maybe once or twice a week. They take any fruit and vegetables they can spare to sell to others. With the cash they get, they can buy essentials for the family. The village has general stores, shops such as butchers, a tailor, a post office. There is likely also to be a primary school, churches, a clinic and local government offices.

Living on a farm in Australia

Most Australians live in the cities. For the farming families that run the cattle and sheep stations of the 'outback' in northern and western Australia, life is very different. Because the land is so dry, little grass grows. This means that the farms have to be very large – some are bigger than counties in the United Kingdom. The farmers move around their land on horseback, or on motorbike, or often with the use of a light aircraft. The farms are too far away from towns for the family to go shopping regularly – instead they buy much of what they need from mail order catalogues.

The climate in these parts of Australia is very hot so buildings remain open at the sides, perhaps with shutters to roll down when it does rain. Children of farming families may not be able to get to a school – instead they use two-way radios to talk to their teachers, and do their lessons at home.

The Flying Doctor Service helps out when people are sick. Light planes land on bumpy

landing strips, and the doctors and nurses on board treat the sick, and take them to hospital if necessary. They treat about 150,000 people a year.

Living in a township in South Africa

South Africa is a multiracial society, where people can live wherever they like. However, many black people who work in the cities cannot afford to move away from the enormous townships. Sometimes these are a long way from the city. Some families have gas and electricity in their township homes – and a tap with cold running water. Houses are usually small, often containing just a living room, a kitchen and a bedroom. There will probably be a fridge and a cooker in the kitchen, there might be a television in the living room, but all the children will have to share a bed.

There is no bathroom, and the toilet is in a shed in the back yard. Often it is just parents and their children living together, but it is common for one or two relatives to live there as well, particularly to look after the children when the parents are at work. Much of the shopping is done at the local spaza – a small local store. The family buys fruit and vegetables at the market. What they most like to eat is mealie (corn) meal porridge. This might accompany slices of sausage for breakfast; for lunch and the evening meal the family eats the porridge with meat and vegetables.

If they have work, the parents have to travel into the city each day. They might do this by train, bus or minibus taxi.

Living on the Caribbean island of St Lucia

The middle of the island is very mountainous, so most people in St Lucia live near the coast. Half the population live in the capital, Castries. Here it is common to see houses built on stilts on the side of the steep hills. Many of the houses are modern with electricity and water supplies. Families are often large with four or more children. Children like to watch television and listen to the radio, but they have to do household chores too, such as cleaning, washing and looking after animals. Families shop at roadside stalls selling fruit and vegetables, at the market or in modern shops.

In the villages, the houses are more simple — maybe just one or two rooms, and water may come from a standpipe. Many of the villagers are farmers, who grow the country's main export crop of bananas and other fruit and vegetables. These days, many people earn a good living from working in the tourist industry. Large cruise ships bring tourists into the fine natural harbour and they stay in one of the many hotels.

The island can be hit by storms and hurricanes between July and November. Torrential rain in a storm in 1994 caused floods and landslides, and swept away roads and bridges.

In their free time, St Lucians love going to the beach and fishing. They like to drink the sweet water that comes from coconuts. Most of the islanders are Roman Catholics and they celebrate Christmas in a big way, with midnight mass, large carol festivals, parties and special food. Carnival, just before Lent, is also a time of celebration, with brightly coloured costumes and dancing in the street.

Living in Papua New Guinea

The scenery is spectacular on this large volcanic island. Traditionally people live in small villages of fewer than 500 people, most of whom are related. Many of the houses are built from local materials, such as bark and bamboo. Often the houses are built on stilts. The villagers have gardens where they grow the food they need, especially taro, yams, sweet potatoes and sago palm. They also grow crops, such as coffee, which they sell for cash. Pigs are highly valued. To have many pigs is a sign of wealth, and they are also roasted at times of celebration. Pigs are often a part of the bride price a man pays for a new wife. It is common for a man to have several wives.

Many people are Christian but they have traditional beliefs too. There are special ceremonies when they decorate their faces and bodies with paint, and put on elaborate headdresses made of bird feathers. The traditional crafts of making canoes, barkcloth (tapa) and pots, and carving religious statues, still continue.

Nowadays, many people are leaving the villages to live in the towns, or to work in the coffee, tea or coconut plantations. On the coast, fishing is also an important occupation. The people of Papua New Guinea love to take part in sports — especially rugby and Australian Rules football. Two important festivals are the Frangipani Festival, which celebrates the blooming of this flower, and Tolai Warwagira, which takes place over two weeks in October or November. There are parades of floats, special sporting events and much singing and dancing.

A village school in Papua New Guinea

chapter 5

the origins of the Commonwealth

To understand the Commonwealth you need to know its history. How has it come about that such a diverse mixture of countries belongs to the same organisation? Why does the Commonwealth use English as its working language? Why is Queen Elizabeth the Head of the Commonwealth? The indisputable fact is that almost all the countries were once a part of what was known as the British Empire, which means they were ruled by Britain. Today, Britain is just one of the Commonwealth's members, with no extra privileges or responsibilities. The process of transformation of empire – at its height Britain controlled 25% of the world's land surface – into the modern Commonwealth is a remarkable one. The story of how this happened is the focus for the next two chapters of this book.

The beginnings: explorers, traders and settlers

To trace the origins of the Commonwealth it is necessary to go back some five hundred years. In the 16th and early 17th centuries, when Elizabeth I and then James I were English monarchs, English adventurers began exploring the world beyond the limits of Europe. Before then, Europeans had travelled across land into Asia, but what was new were their voyages across the oceans. It was not only the English who were turning their attention to the world beyond the immediate horizon – explorers and adventurers from Portugal, Spain and Holland were doing the same thing.

The long and remarkable voyages of these men took the small sailing ships of the time across the Atlantic, to the far north of Canada, around the southernmost tip of South America, into the Pacific, and around the Cape of Good Hope to reach India and the islands of the East Indies (now Indonesia).

The explorers were followed by other British people who saw exciting opportunities in the new lands and new sea routes.

- John Cabot sailed from Bristol in 1497, and found the area of North America which came to be called 'Newfoundland'. By the 1570s, fishermen from the south-west of England were regularly spending their summers in Newfoundland, returning to England with their salted cod before the winter.

- A group of merchants came together in 1600 and formed the East India Company. The object of this company was to trade with India and the East Indies. The items the traders most valued were initially spices – as precious as gold in Europe at the time and used for food, cosmetics and medicines. Other valuable items of trade were tea, fine china, and beautiful fabrics.

- The first British colony in North America was started in 1607. This was at Jamestown. Both here and then elsewhere in North America and some West Indian islands, tobacco was grown to export to Europe. Smoking had recently become a fashionable occupation there.

• Some people sailed to the new lands because they wanted the freedom to worship God as they wished. This was a powerful motive for settlement on the eastern coasts of North America.

• In 1688 King Charles II gave the Hudson Bay Company the right to trade in a large part of Canada – it amounted to about 40% of the land area. It was the trade in furs which was the driving force of this company.

There were others who were given no choice in the matter but who were taken to the new lands as a punishment. In the 18th century, about 30,000 people were 'transported' to North America, having been convicted of crimes. Transportation was an alternative to hanging – and was a standard punishment for even small offences, such as stealing a loaf of bread. Thus by 1700, Britain had colonies in North America and the West Indies, and its trading companies were busy exploiting the riches of India and the frozen wastes of Canada.

The slave trade

It was in the 17th century that this terrible trade began. The plantation owners of the West Indies had realised that sugar was more suited to their climate than tobacco. The cultivation of sugar, however, needed many workers. The indigenous people of the West Indies (the Amerindians) were not considered suitable for such work and their numbers anyway had been reduced by diseases brought by the Europeans. So the plantation owners looked overseas.

During the 17th century European traders began doing business with the people on the coasts of West and Central Africa. These traders started to transport people from Africa across the Atlantic to work in the sugar plantations. The people that were taken, however, had no choice in the matter – they were slaves who were bought and sold like any other items of trade. The British established what became known as the triangular trade. The ships carried their sick and unhappy cargoes across the Atlantic. Many died in the wretched conditions on the slave ships. Once arrived in the West Indies, they were sold to plantation owners. The ships then carried sugar back across the Atlantic to be sold in Europe.

In Britain the ships would load up with the guns, metal goods and textiles which were taken to West Africa to exchange for the slaves. The whole business was highly profitable and many British fortunes were made.

By the mid-1700s, about 70,000 slaves a year were being taken across the Atlantic, half of them in British ships. It is estimated that in total some 4 million Africans were sold into slavery by British traders. They were either sold to British colonies in the West Indies or were sold to other colonies in North America.

Canada
Newfoundland
EUROPE
NORTH AMERICA
sugar
the triangular trade
guns, metal goods and textiles
WEST INDIES
slaves
Pacific Ocean
SOUTH AMERICA
AFRICA
Atlantic Ocean

West African empires

Long before the 17th century, there had been several powerful empires in the interior of West Africa. The rulers of these states were extremely wealthy, their riches being based on trade across the Sahara with North Africa. This is what one observer wrote about the ancient kingdom of Ghana, four hundred years before the first Portuguese explorers found their way around the coast of Africa in the 15th century:

'When he gives audience to his people, to listen to their complaints ... he sits in a pavilion around which stand ten pages holding shields and gold-mounted swords: and on his right hand are the princes of his empire, splendidly clad and with gold plaited into their hair ... The gate of the chamber is guarded by dogs of an excellent breed, who never leave the king's seat: they wear collars of gold and silver.'

(Basil Davidson, *The African Past*, 1964)

The British traders did not capture the slaves themselves. They worked through African chiefs who wanted the goods the British brought, and were prepared to raid their enemies' territories to capture new slaves.

The descendants of the African slaves who were taken across the Atlantic now make up the black population of the United States, and form the largest ethnic group in most Caribbean islands.

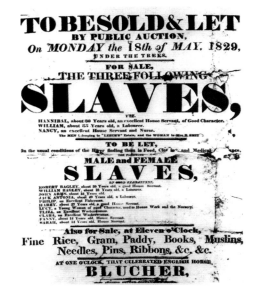

'They came again every now and then for a month, as long as they could find people to carry away. They sold all they carried away, to be slaves. They took away brothers, and sisters, and husbands and wives; they did not care about this. They were sold for cloth or gunpowder, sometimes for salt or guns.' **(Louis Asa-Asa describes a slave raid in 1831)**

Expansion of the Empire

For the best part of a century British ships sailed all over the world, carrying goods, slaves and settlers. The sugar islands continued to prosper, the East India Company took control of parts of India, and British people arrived in a totally new continent – Australasia. During the 18th century the British navy came to dominate the world, with its 400 ships and 80,000 sailors – a dominance which continued until the beginning of the 20th century.

It was a century of warfare too, with the main enemy being the French. The two countries were at war on and off for the best part of 125 years. The wars were partly about acquiring colonies. Much of the action was played out in the colonies – some island colonies changed hands several times.

North America

Relations between Britain and its American colonies became increasingly difficult. The central issue was one of taxation. The American colonies did not think it was fair that they should pay taxes to Britain. In 1776, the American colonies declared their independence. For six years, the British tried to keep control of these troublesome colonies but had to admit defeat in 1782 – and thus the United States of America was born.

People in North America who were loyal to the British crown fled northwards over the border to Canada. In 1759 General James Wolfe had captured the French city of Quebec giving the British control of French-speaking people in the area. They were joined by the loyalists. So instead of controlling a narrow strip of shoreline in North America, the British found themselves controlling the vast land mass of Canada, which runs from east to west across North America.

Australia

In 1768-79 Captain James Cook led three voyages to the South Pacific. These voyages brought the British into contact with the huge land of Australia. Taking troublesome people to the other side of the world appealed to the British, especially since criminals could not be transported to America any more. In 1788 the first convict colony was established at Botany Bay in Australia – 737 men, women and children. In total, 162,000 convicts were sent to Australia before the practice ended in 1868. Most settled in Australia once they were free.

The British viewed Australia as an empty land, disregarding the rights of the aboriginal peoples. They hunted these people down. Many aborigines were killed or died of the new diseases brought by the white men. It is only now that the ancient land rights of the aboriginal peoples are being recognised.

India

In India, the East India Company was becoming more aggressive. Where Indian states would not co-operate, they took them over. By the 1780s the company ruled over 20 million Indians. (See 'India: the Jewel in the Crown' on page 41.)

The height of Empire

In 1815 a long period of European warfare ended. Around the world, agreements were made concerning the ownership of colonies, and Britain took over control of Cape Colony (later South Africa).

South Africa

A Dutch company settled at the Cape in the mid-17th century. They defeated the indigenous inhabitants and decided to import slaves. These came from the East Indies and the east coast of Africa. Early on in the colony's history some white farmers moved into the interior of the Cape, taking their slaves with them. There were constant disagreements between these farmers and the officials of the Dutch East India Company.

The British meanwhile had seen the error of their ways where slavery was concerned. Led by Christian evangelists, a successful campaign was launched to end both the slave trade, and slavery itself. The British officials at the Cape were keen to help slaves achieve their freedom. This became a source of bitterness between the British and the Dutch farmers, who moved ever further into the interior, to be free of British control. As they did so, they came into conflict with some powerful groups of Africans. This led to a prolonged period of war.

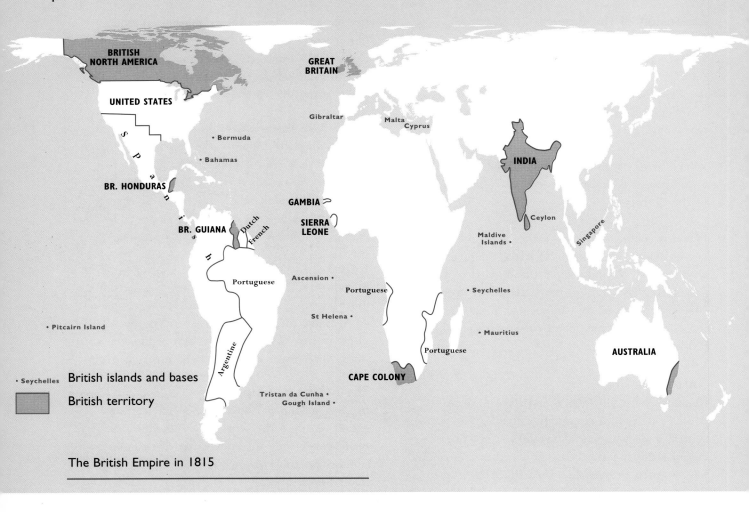

British islands and bases

British territory

The British Empire in 1815

The conflict between British and Boers (Dutch farmers) continued throughout the 19th century, culminating in a bitter war fought between 1899 and 1902. The British won that war, but the Boers (or Afrikaners as they came to be called) were able to control the colony from 1910.

Changing views of Empire

In the first 300 years of the British Empire the prime motive behind expansion had been making money through trade. However, in the 19th century the British developed loftier views about their colonial responsibilities.

Thomas Buxton was a British MP, and a campaigner to end slavery. In 1837 he said: 'The British Empire has been singularly blessed by Providence … Can we suppose otherwise than that it is our office to carry civilisation and humanity, peace and good government, and above all, knowledge of the true God, to the uttermost ends of the Earth?'

Inspired by this view, British Christian missionaries took themselves to remote parts of the Empire to spread the word of the Lord. They took with them all the arrogant preconceptions of the Victorian age about what constituted 'civilisation'. They condemned the houses, the form of dress, the customs, the medicine of the people with whom they worked. Instead they offered a Victorian way of life and provided a Christian education, teaching their converts to read the Bible.

In most areas of Africa the missionaries were not very successful. The number of people who became converted to Christianity remained small. However, the missionaries played their part in the spread of empire.

'At times, especially in the final quarter of the [19th] century, European missionaries appealed to their home governments for various degrees of political or military "protection". This was usually in the face of local political conflict which threatened the safety of their missions. Nevertheless, when European governments responded positively to these appeals, it was usually due more to their own wider strategic and commercial interests.'

(Kevin Shillington, *History of Africa*, Macmillan, 1995)

Victorian missionaries and their African converts

Moshoeshoe and Lesotho

During the time of war in Southern Africa (see page 38) one individual stands out as a man of peace. This was Moshoeshoe, the leader of the Sotho people. There was so much insecurity in the area that in 1824 he led his people to safety across 120 kilometres of mountains in the depths of winter. The refuge he chose was Thaba Bosiu. This was a flat-topped mountain, where the summit was surrounded by overhanging cliffs and there was fresh water. From here

Moshoeshoe asserted control over the region by his hospitality, clever marriage alliances, and buying the loyalty of those he had defeated by granting them cattle to look after. One of the things he said was: 'Peace is like the rain which makes the grass grow, while war is like the wind which dries it up'. By his wise actions, Moshoeshoe founded the small mountain kingdom of Lesotho.

Effects of industrialisation

At the end of the 18th century a process started which was to transform life in Britain. A series of technological breakthroughs by British scientists and engineers led to the industrial revolution. Businessmen built factories in the cities where the new machines, powered by coal, made large-scale production possible. The factories needed labour. People from the countryside poured into the towns and cities to take the jobs which were now on offer, even though working conditions and pay were wretched. Britain was the first country to industrialise, and it was making more goods than could be sold in the home market — overseas markets were needed.

The industrial revolution transformed transport too. Across Britain a network of railways was built at astonishing speed. The British pioneered new technology in the 19th century so that the sailing ships of the past were replaced by much faster steamships. Towards the end of the century the British were building two-thirds of the world's ships, thus ensuring the continuation of British domination of the high seas. The combination of industrialisation and new, faster forms of transport ensured British domination of the world's trade. The British developed a system of trade within the Empire which was vastly profitable to the factory owners of Britain, but which was of little benefit to the people of the colonies. Raw cotton was shipped from India to England where it was processed in the cotton mills of Lancashire; the cotton cloth was then taken back to India to be sold. Wool from Australia was made into blankets in the mills of Yorkshire, and taken back to Australia to be sold.

Emigration and settlement

The century saw a rapid rise in emigration, as British people (and Irish) sailed to the new territories to make a new life. There was a flood of emigrants after 1815 when unemployment in Britain was high. About 6 million British people emigrated to Canada, Australia and New Zealand between 1815 and 1914. They were encouraged to do so by offers of free passages. Smaller number of British settlers sailed to South Africa.

The scramble for Africa

Until the end of the 19th century British

possessions in Sub-Saharan Africa were limited to South Africa and two settlements for freed slaves at Bathurst (now Banjul) and Freetown on the coast of West Africa. The British government did not want more colonies in Africa — colonies were expensive to run. They were happy to let explorers, traders and missionaries open up new parts of the continent. Yet by 1900 virtually the whole of Africa south of the Sahara had been carved up into colonies, many of them ruled by the British. What caused this dramatic change in thinking?

At the end of the 19th century British industrial dominance was being challenged, especially by Germany and the United States of America. This meant that Britain faced more competition in the search for new markets for its manufactured goods. More important than economic factors however were those of politics. Other European countries — Germany, France, Portugal and Belgium — began looking at Africa both as a possible source of raw materials and to increase prestige. There were strategic considerations too — one motive for taking over territories in East Africa was to protect the route to India.

India the Jewel in the Crown

India was always the most precious of Britain's overseas possessions. Trade with the sub-continent was highly profitable, fine cotton cloth becoming the most important export.

When the East India Company first operated, India was divided into many different states, most controlled by princes. To further their commercial interests, the East India Company made alliances with some princes, fought wars against others. By the middle of the 19th century the company controlled most of India, although its officials had little understanding of what mattered to their millions of subjects. They decided, for example, that it should be compulsory for Indians to become Christian. Ignorance of Indian religious customs led to the Indian Mutiny of 1857, when both Muslim and Hindu soldiers reacted violently to being issued with cartridges greased with animal fats.

The mutiny turned into a savage war, which dragged on for two years. The Indian rebels captured Delhi and besieged Lucknow. Both sides murdered women and children. So shocked were the British, that when extra troops arrived from Britain, they punished those who had taken part in the uprising with unusual cruelty. The Indians referred to this time as 'The Devil's Wind':

'The first ten of the prisoners were lashed to the guns, the artillery officer waved his sword, you heard the roar of the guns, and above the smoke you saw legs, arms and heads flying in all directions. Since that time we have had an execution parade once or twice a week, and such is the force of habit we now think little of them'. (Eyewitness quoted in Jan Morris, *Pax Britannica*, Faber, 1968)

These events showed that the East India Company was no longer capable of governing India. Instead, the British government took over the administration of India, establishing a system of government which was known as the Raj. Queen Victoria became the Empress of India; a Viceroy ruled India on her behalf. British civil servants ran the administration and half the British army was stationed in India.

Taking tea in nineteenth-century India

At the same time, there were individuals working in Africa who were dedicated to the spread of empire – inspired by the wish to spread 'civilisation' which typified the Victorian age. Cecil Rhodes dreamed of the British ruling Africa 'from the Cape to Cairo'. To further this aim he led a group of settlers into Central Africa, fought against the Africans there and began the colony of Rhodesia (now Zimbabwe).

Once the scramble began, the British had to join in. British officials negotiated treaties with chiefs to acquire rights over their land. (There was a basic misunderstanding here: the British thought the chiefs were giving them permission to do what they liked with their land; in fact the lands belonged to the people and could not be given away.) British troops raced against the French to control strategic points. Force was frequently used. African armies often fought bravely, but the superior weaponry of the British usually won the day. The Maxim-gun, which was the first mobile modern machinegun, was particularly lethal.

In 1884, there was a conference in Berlin. European governments drew lines on the map of Africa and distributed the lands amongst themselves. Often the lines were drawn straight across the map, dividing ethnic groups into two, or joining traditional enemies into one colony. Within the space of 20 years or so, the British Empire had dramatically increased in size.

A British poet, Hilaire Belloc, who opposed the British imperial conquests, wrote:

'Whatever happens we have got
The Maxim-gun and they have not'.

African resistance

Often, there was rivalry amongst the different African ethnic groups. This made it difficult for them to unite against the European invaders. However, there were several places where African peoples put up a determined resistance.

Southern Africa
In the 1870s the Zulu people of Southern Africa won a famous victory against the British at Isandhlwana, and it took eight months of campaigning and thousands of British reinforcements before the Zulus were finally defeated.

West Africa
Samori Touré led an army of 30,000 against the French in the interior of West Africa in the 1880s.

The Asante people nearly succeeded in throwing the British out of what is now Ghana in 1900.

East Africa
The Maji-Maji rebellion of the early 1900s saw widespread resistance to German colonial rule in what is now Tanzania.

The Diamond Jubilee of Queen Victoria

In 1897 Queen Victoria had been on the throne for 60 years. She was head of the largest empire in the history of the world. It spread over nearly a quarter of the land mass of the world, and a quarter of its population. The occasion was marked by an enormous celebration in London, an affirmation of imperialism. Fifty thousand troops took part in the procession, coming from every corner of the Empire (below).

However, this mood of self-congratulation did not last. As the new century dawned, it was soon clear that the Empire was beginning to crumble.

'The 19th century had been pre-eminently Britain's century, and the British saw themselves still as top dogs. ... they had seemed to be arbiters of the world's affairs ... ringing the earth with railways and submarine cables, lending money everywhere, peopling the empty places with men of British stock, grandly revenging wrongs, emancipating slaves, winning wars, discovering unknown lakes, putting down mutinies ... and building bigger and faster battleships.'
(Jan Morris, *Pax Britannica*, Faber, 1968)

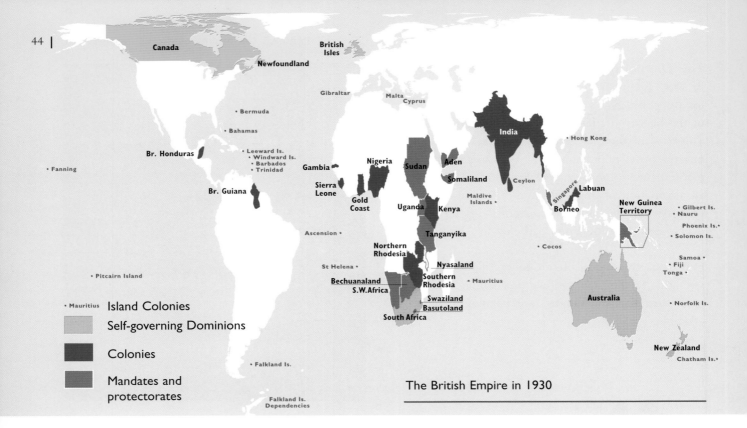

Island Colonies

Self-governing Dominions

Colonies

Mandates and protectorates

The British Empire in 1930

The twentieth century – the end of empire

There was still some expansion to come. At the end of the First World War, Britain took on the administration of some colonies which had previously been run by countries defeated in the war. For example, it took over Tanganyika (now Tanzania) which before the war had been controlled by Germany. In 1920 the Empire was at its height.

At the beginning of the 20th century, the Empire was made up of three kinds of colony. There were the lands to which British people had emigrated – Canada, Australia, New Zealand and South Africa. There was India – in a category of its own. And there were the others – the colonies in Africa, Asia, South Pacific, the Caribbean. These included strings of islands, sometimes quite remote from anywhere else, such as St Helena and Ascension in the South Atlantic. The British had taken control of these small places as useful stopping places for their ships. British people only made up 12% of the peoples of the Empire. But all peoples had the English monarch as their head of state, used the English language for official purposes and for education, and adopted the English legal system.

The Dominions

The lands where British people had settled in large numbers wanted to run their own affairs. From 1897 until 1945 the leaders of these countries met regularly at Imperial Conferences. After discussion about the status of these countries the word 'dominion' began to be used. In 1926 the terms of Dominion status were agreed in the Balfour Report. These countries and Britain were described as: ' … *autonomous communities within the British Empire, equal in status, in no way subordinate one to another in any aspect of their domestic or external affairs, though united by a common allegiance to the Crown, and freely associated as members of the British Commonwealth of Nations*'.

In 1931 the British Parliament passed the Statute of Westminster which allowed the Dominions to become independent nations.

The colonies

The colonies were not thought of as being able to run their own affairs. Small groups of British officials administered enormous areas, imposing British justice, keeping law and order and charging taxes. Railways were built from the coasts into the interior: in Kenya the railway meant white settlers could travel to the good farming lands in the highlands; often the railways were used to bring crops to the coast for export. The building of schools and hospitals was often left to the missionaries.

Mahatma Gandhi

Gandhi was one of the world's most remarkable leaders. He trained as a lawyer and worked for an Indian firm in South Africa for 21 years.

There he campaigned on behalf of the Indian community, developing his methods of non-violent protest. Once back in India, Gandhi was greatly affected by the massacre of Amritsar in 1919 when hundreds of nationalist demonstrators were killed by British troops. Shortly afterwards he became the leader of the Indian National Congress. He organised protests against British rule, and led boycotts of British goods. Gandhi was frequently imprisoned by the British authorities. His final spell of imprisonment was in 1942-44, when he led the 'Quit India' movement. Gandhi believed in simple living, and did not think that

India should become an industrial country. He himself spun thread and made cloth for his own clothes. He tried hard to work with the Muslim League, and strongly opposed the idea of partition. He was assassinated by a Hindu fanatic in 1948, who thought Gandhi's opposition to partition meant that he was pro-Muslim.

India

Although large numbers of Indian troops fought for Britain in both world wars, there was great unrest in that country. By 1906 there were two powerful political parties in India: the Indian National Congress, which came to represent the Hindu people of India (who made up about 80% of the population); and the All-India Muslim League which represented the Muslims (who made up about 20%).

Both parties wanted India to be able to govern itself, just as the Dominions were doing. However the British were very reluctant to give up control of India. Mahatma Gandhi became leader of the Indian National Congress in the 1920s and began a non-violent campaign for independence.

The Congress objected to being brought into the Second World War without any consultation and began a 'Quit India' movement. The demand for independence was becoming so powerful that the British had to make concessions.

However, rivalry between the two parties, and the two religions, made independence difficult. The Muslims mostly lived in the north-west and north-east of India, so the League began asking for its own separate Muslim state in those areas. Britain decided India would have to be divided to form the new states of Pakistan and India. Both countries became independent in 1947. Immediately afterwards there was chaos, as followers of the different religions tried to reach their new homes. There was terrible violence, and about a million people died. The British did little or nothing to prevent or stop the killing.

The world wars

Britain went to war against Germany in 1914 and again in 1939. In 1914, there was no question but that the entire Empire was also at war. Nearly 7 million British soldiers took part in the First World War; a further million came from the Dominions; and a million men in India volunteered to take part. Troops also fought for Britain from East and West Africa, from the Caribbean, Egypt and Mauritius.

In 1939, the Dominions were not compelled to follow Britain into war. Australia and New Zealand regarded themselves as bound by the British declaration of war. The issue was debated in Canada and South Africa but they soon took the decision to go to war as well. Three million troops from all over the 'British Commonwealth of Nations' fought in the war. Two million of these came from India.

When Japan entered the war, the countries in the Pacific region were at risk of attack. The Australians fought the Japanese in Papua New Guinea to stave off an attack on Australia – the north coast of Australia experienced over 100 air raids. Malaya, Singapore, Burma and Hong Kong – all British territories – were captured by the Japanese and thousands were killed, imprisoned or enslaved.

A new form of association

Indian independence led to a profound change in the British Commonwealth. After independence, India was led by Jawaharlal Nehru. He agreed to India having Dominion status, but his aim was to make India a republic, so that the British monarch would not be its head of state. He wanted, however, to keep the association with Britain, the Dominions and the rest of the Empire. As he said:

'We join the Commonwealth obviously because we think it is beneficial to us and to certain causes in the world that we wish to advance. The other countries of the Commonwealth want us to remain, because they think it is beneficial to them ... In a world where there are so many disruptive forces at work, where we are often at the verge of war, I think it is not a safe thing to encourage the breaking up of any association that one has ... it is better to keep a co-operative association going which may do good in this world rather than break it.'

The other countries of the British Commonwealth took some time to agree to a republic joining the association. Eventually, however, it was agreed that India could join. As part of this agreement, the title 'British Commonwealth of Nations' was dropped and India became a republic within the Commonwealth. This happened in 1949 – a turning point in the history of the Commonwealth.

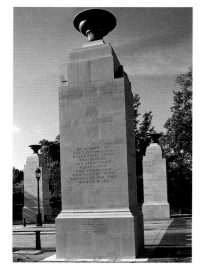

Gates commemorating those who gave their lives in Asia in two world wars

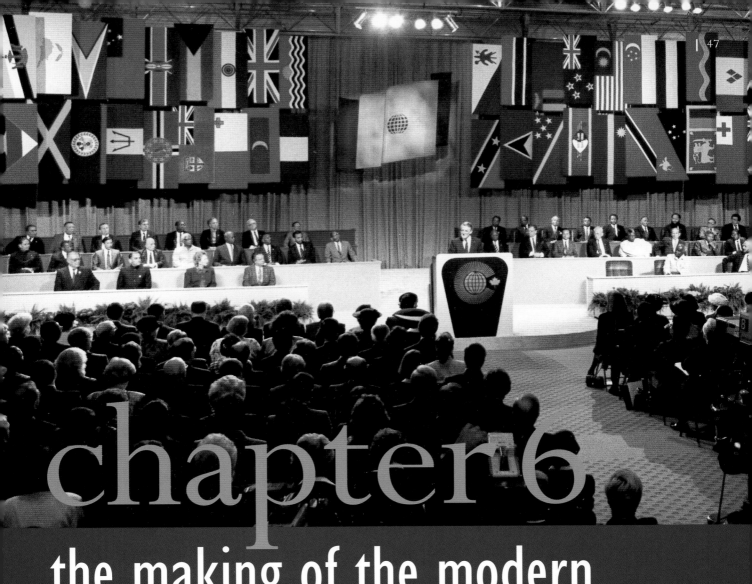

chapter 6

the making of the modern Commonwealth

As we saw in the last chapter, 1949 marked an important turning point in the history of the Commonwealth. With the entry of India, Pakistan and then Ceylon (now Sri Lanka), the days of its being a white man's club were over. Instead it was becoming a meeting point for different races. There was a change in style as well. Instead of Imperial Conferences, there were Prime Ministers' Meetings. These were private, informal affairs. There were no votes on formal resolutions – instead the leaders exchanged views and discussed topics until they were broadly in agreement, i.e. until consensus had been reached. This is still the style of Commonwealth meetings.

In 1948 there were eight countries in the Commonwealth – Australia, Canada, New Zealand, South Africa, United Kingdom, India, Pakistan and Ceylon. No-one could have predicted that just over 20 years later, the Commonwealth would have expanded to include nearly 30 countries. The post-war world was a profoundly changed one: the rise of nationalist feelings meant that Britain could not continue to govern a large number of colonies.

The winds of change

Nowhere was this more evident than in Africa. Those colonies, which had been so arbitrarily made by drawing lines on a map, were now becoming nations; the people were beginning to feel a sense of unity. New leaders, often educated in Britain or the United States, started political parties. These parties campaigned for independence. The Prime Minister of Britain, Harold Macmillan, spoke of the rise of national consciousness in a speech he made in Africa in 1960: 'The most striking of all the impressions I have formed since I left London a month ago is of this African national consciousness. In different places it may take different forms, but it is happening everywhere. The wind of change is blowing through the continent'.

By 1970, most British colonies in Africa had become independent nations. This goal was sometimes only achieved through violence, and the imprisonment of African political leaders by the British authorities was not uncommon. However, in those colonies where few white people had settled, the transition to independence was usually relatively straightforward.

The West African colony of Gold Coast, now Ghana, set the pattern. It became independent in 1957. The other British colonies in West Africa soon followed Ghana's example: the huge country of Nigeria became independent in 1960, Sierra Leone followed suit in 1961 and The Gambia in 1965.

In East Africa, the former colonies of Tanganyika (now Tanzania) and Uganda became independent in 1961 and 1962 respectively. The transition towards independence in Kenya was more painful since many Europeans and Asians had settled there and feared they would lose their lands. For some years the Mau Mau, a secret society, fought against the British. The British imprisoned Jomo Kenyatta, the main African leader, declared a state of emergency and flew in large numbers of troops. However, Kenya became the third of the former British colonies in East Africa to win its freedom in 1963, with Kenyatta as its Prime Minister.

The end of empire – the beginnings of equal status

The 1960s saw the tide of independence spread across the old empire. Six more countries in Africa – Botswana, Lesotho, Mauritius, Malawi, Swaziland and Zambia – achieved independence within the decade. By 1970 most of the larger Caribbean islands were independent, as well as British Guiana (now Guyana). Malaya (later Malaysia) had become independent in 1957 and Singapore, Cyprus and Malta soon followed suit.

In the 1970s, it was the turn of smaller Caribbean islands and countries in the South Pacific to become independent of British rule. A few small territories, such as Bermuda and the Falkland Islands, chose to remain British colonies.

Remarkably, most of these independent countries chose to join the Commonwealth. This was something new – an empire replaced by a voluntary association of states which are all regarded as equal. In this association, Britain was just one of the members – it had no special rights, privileges or responsibilities. Yet it was because of the shared history and language that Commonwealth leaders were able to talk to each other in a frank and informal way.

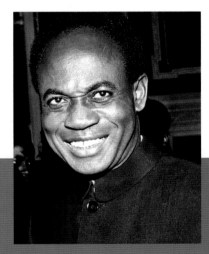

In 1961, Kwame Nkrumah gave a speech on freedom in Africa:

Kwame Nkrumah

Kwame Nkrumah, a charismatic and able man, returned from Europe to the Gold Coast (now Ghana). In 1949 he became the leader of the Convention People's Party. The party began to campaign for independence. There were demonstrations against British rule which became violent. The British reacted by putting Nkrumah in prison. In 1951 there were elections and Nkrumah's party won most of the seats. The British realised that independence had to come. Nkrumah came out of prison to become Prime Minister. For some years, British advisers assisted the African ministers prepare for independence and in 1957 the new independent nation of Ghana was born.

'For centuries, Europeans dominated the African continent. The white man arrogated to himself the right to rule and to be obeyed by the non-white; his mission, he claimed, was to 'civilise' Africa. Under this cloak, the Europeans robbed the continent of vast riches and inflicted unimaginable suffering on the African people.

All this makes a sad story, but now we must be prepared to bury the past with its unpleasant memories and look to the future. All we ask of the former colonial powers is their goodwill and co-operation to remedy past mistakes and injustices and to grant independence to the colonies in Africa.'

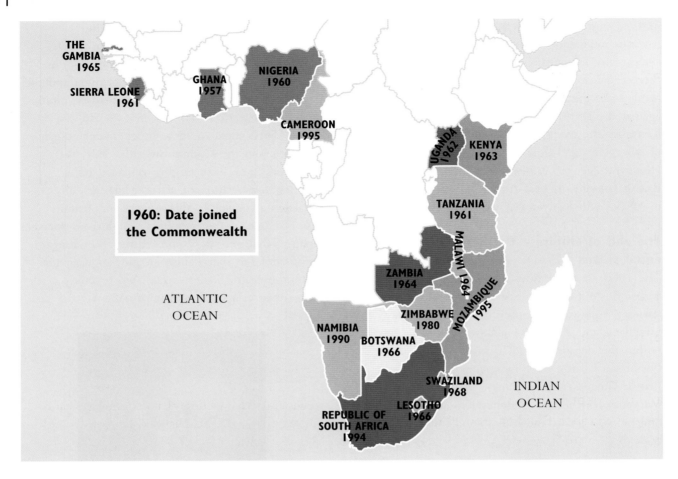

THE
GAMBIA
1965

SIERRA LEONE
1961

GHANA
1957

NIGERIA
1960

CAMEROON
1995

UGANDA
1962

KENYA
1963

TANZANIA
1961

MALAWI 1964

ZAMBIA
1964

MOZAMBIQUE 1995

1960: Date joined
the Commonwealth

ATLANTIC
OCEAN

ZIMBABWE
1980

NAMIBIA
1990

BOTSWANA
1966

SWAZILAND
1968

INDIAN
OCEAN

LESOTHO
1966

REPUBLIC OF
SOUTH AFRICA
1994

The Commonwealth and Southern Africa

The 20 years after 1960 were difficult ones for
the Commonwealth. The white governments
of Southern Rhodesia and South Africa were
imposing racial policies which discriminated
against the majority of their citizens. Whenever
Commonwealth leaders met they argued about
what should be done about these countries.
There were times when it looked as if Southern
Africa would tear the Commonwealth apart.

Southern Rhodesia

The colony of Southern Rhodesia was started by
Cecil Rhodes. Its climate and good agricultural
land attracted many European settlers. Southern
Rhodesia was never run from Britain – instead
it was governed until 1923 by the British South
Africa Company. For a long time, the British
government was happy to let the white settlers
run the country as they chose – even though
they made up only 5% of the population, the
remaining 95% being black.

However, as British colonies further north in
Africa moved towards independence, the mood

changed. The white settlers wanted independence
for their country too, but the British government
insisted that this could only happen if the
political rights of the black majority were
protected. The British said that black citizens
should have at least one-third of the seats in
parliament, and that there should be progress
towards majority rule. Majority rule meant
giving all adults the vote, and would inevitably
mean a black government. The white
government of Rhodesia responded by giving
Africans just 15 out of 65 seats and by refusing
to consider majority rule.

The following passage is from a story written by
Charles Mungoshi, a leading Zimbabwean writer.
In it he is describing what life was like in his
country in the 1960s. This story was banned
by the white government.

Skyline today; Harare, Zimbabwe

'When they were tired of going round the factories and shops in search of jobs, the boys went to the tall buildings at the heart of the city for their daily ride in the lifts. It was the only fun they had and it made them forget a little their burning bellies and tired feet.

Pearl Assurance Building, one of the tallest buildings in the city, had a guard at the wide entrance.

"Can I help you?" the guard asked.

"We would like to go up."

"Floor?"

"Tenth"

The guard looked at them suspiciously and then dismissed them with a flick of the hand.

"You are not allowed up there. There has been much stealing up there lately," the guard said.

"We are not thieves."

The guard's eyes swept over their heads and he dismissed them from his attention.

"Go away, boys."

The boys turned to go. They passed two European boys of their own age. Looking back, the boys saw the guard take off his cap to the Europeans who did not answer him and quickly entered the lift and disappeared.'

(Adapted from *Coming of the Dry Season*, OUP/Zimbabwe Publishing House, 1972)

The white government of Rhodesia made membership of the two main black political parties illegal, and imprisoned African leaders. When the British government continued to refuse his requests for independence, the Prime Minister, Ian Smith, declared Rhodesia independent anyway. This Unilateral Declaration of Independence (UDI) happened in November 1965.

Impact on the Commonwealth

The issue of Rhodesia caused bitter divisions among Commonwealth members, the association tending to split along racial lines. The African members were particularly outraged. The Caribbean and Asian members sided with the new African members – and Canada also wanted Britain to insist on majority rule. Ghana and Nigeria wanted the British to send troops to Rhodesia; the leader of newly independent Zambia, Kenneth Kaunda, talked of 'throwing Britain out of the Commonwealth'. In 1966, when a special meeting of the Commonwealth leaders met in Lagos, Nigeria, it began to look as if the Commonwealth would not survive.

Britain refused to send troops but condemned UDI and stopped buying Rhodesian tobacco and sugar. Most countries imposed sanctions on Rhodesia, cutting off its trade. However, sanctions had only a limited effect.

Negotiating a settlement in 1979

Civil war began in Rhodesia, with different black groups fighting against the white government forces. It took 15 years before the struggle for freedom was won. The Commonwealth Secretary-General of the time, Sonny Ramphal, and the presidents of Zambia and Tanzania worked hard to bring the different black groups to the negotiating table. The settlement led to a general election, based on majority rule, in which Robert Mugabe won an overwhelming number of seats. Zimbabwe became independent in 1980, and joined the Commonwealth.

The Commonwealth had survived, and had made its opposition to racial discrimination clear. The Canadians had played an important role in drafting the communiqué at the end of the Prime Ministers' Meeting of 1964. The opening section of this communiqué contained a declaration of support for racial equality and opposition to discrimination.

South Africa

By the 1980s, it was South Africa which was preoccupying the leaders of the Commonwealth. This country had actually left the Commonwealth in 1961. Run by Afrikaners, the South African government had racist policies which were totally unacceptable to the rest of the Commonwealth. Under its policies of apartheid (meaning 'separation'), the black people of South Africa were told where they could live and work. They had to live far away from the white people of South Africa. This meant that many of them had to travel long distances each day from where they lived to where they worked – which was in the white cities, or on the white farms. They had no political rights, except in ethnic homelands which were on poor land and where few people wanted to live. Each black person had to carry a pass book, and had to use separate buses, schools and hospitals, where facilities were poor. Black leaders, such as Nelson Mandela, were imprisoned.

Impact on Commonwealth

With the problem of Zimbabwe now solved, the racist regime of South Africa stood out even more as an affront against humanity. Sonny Ramphal, the Secretary-General, adopted the campaign against apartheid as his own personal crusade. With its commitment to racial equality and democracy, how could the Commonwealth stand aside from the struggles of the people of South Africa?

The Soweto uprising, 1976

In 1971, a student called Steve Biko called on black people in South Africa to unite to fight against white racism:

'*Black consciousness ... seeks to infuse the black community with a new-found pride in themselves, their efforts, their value systems, their culture, their religion and their outlook to life ... Blacks no longer seek to reform the system because so doing implies acceptance of the major points around which the system revolves. Blacks are out to completely transform the system and to make of it what they wish*'.

In 1976, inspired by words like these, thousands of school children from the black township of Soweto poured into the streets. They demonstrated against having to learn the Afrikaans language. This was the language of the Afrikaner people, who had imposed the hated policy of apartheid on the land. A 13-year-old girl was shot by the police. Throughout the country, black students rose in revolt. The police responded by killing almost 600 people, 134 of whom were under 18. Steve Biko was arrested and died of brain damage after being beaten by the police. Thousands of young black South Africans fled over the borders to join military training camps, intent on bringing war against the white oppressors of their country.

Five Commonwealth countries in Southern Africa committed themselves to ending apartheid. These 'front-line states' of Botswana, Swaziland, Tanzania, Zambia and Zimbabwe, were joined by the countries of Mozambique and Angola in 1975. These two countries had just become independent of Portuguese rule.

Most of the Commonwealth countries wanted to impose strict sanctions against South Africa, cutting off all trade and investment. Britain, with Margaret Thatcher as its Prime Minister, disagreed. The communiqués of the Commonwealth Heads of Government Meetings of 1987 and 1989 restated the Commonwealth position, adding the words 'with the exception of Britain'.

The 1985 Commonwealth Heads of Government Meeting appointed an Eminent Persons Group, headed by a former prime minister of Australia and a former head of state of Nigeria. This group visited South Africa and was able to open up some lines of communication between the various factions there. Commonwealth pressure played a part in improving the situation and by 1991, some political prisoners were being released in South Africa, and opposition political parties were emerging.

The end of apartheid

As the 1990s began, there were dramatic changes in South Africa. The Afrikaner Prime Minister, F W de Klerk, released Nelson Mandela from prison after 27 years. The two men negotiated a new political settlement for the country. In 1994, for the first time, every adult in South Africa, regardless of their ethnic group, was allowed to vote. The queues outside polling stations stretched for miles (see above). A democratic government was elected, Mandela (left) became President and South Africa rejoined the Commonwealth after a break of 33 years.

The modern Commonwealth

Despite the problems of Southern Africa, the Commonwealth had survived. In fact those troubles had helped to strengthen the Commonwealth's commitment to racial equality. They had also shown that the association was no longer focused on Britain – what held the member countries together was a belief in the same set of values, not their colonial past.

The Commonwealth Secretariat

Despite that, it made sense for the headquarters of the Commonwealth to be based in London. All the Commonwealth countries had diplomatic missions in London, and communications between the British capital and Commonwealth capitals were good. The idea of having such a headquarters was first suggested in the late 1950s. In 1959 the Queen agreed that one of her palaces, Marlborough House (see above), could be used as a Commonwealth centre. In 1965, a Secretariat was set up there, to co-ordinate the activities of the Commonwealth.

To start with, Marlborough House was used for Prime Ministers' Meetings but in 1971 the practice was established of holding what were then called Commonwealth Heads of Government Meetings (CHOGMs) in different Commonwealth countries. That of 1971 was held in Singapore.

The Commonwealth Secretariat is not a British organisation. It is multinational. Senior staff are seconded from different Commonwealth countries for limited periods. (For further information on the Secretariat and the structure of the Commonwealth see Chapter 10.)

The Singapore Declaration of 1971

In 1971, the first Commonwealth Heads of Government Meeting was held at Singapore. The majority of members were leaders of developing countries. South Africa was on the agenda because Commonwealth African leaders accused Britain of selling arms to the apartheid regime. Kenneth Kaunda, the leader of Zambia, drafted a declaration of principles, his intention being to bind the association together and to prevent separate British action. This declaration was agreed by the heads of government and has become the document which underpins the modern Commonwealth.

The Singapore Declaration states support for:
- peace and order
- the rule of international law
- the liberty and equality of each individual
- international co-operation

and opposition to:
- racial discrimination (referred to as 'a dangerous sickness')
- the oppression of one group of people by another
- the wide gap between rich and poor

To show their determination to reduce the gap between rich and poor, the heads of government, at the same meeting in Singapore, agreed to set up the Commonwealth Fund for Technical Co-operation (CFTC). The purpose of this fund was to reduce poverty in the Commonwealth (see page 64 for details of work done by CFTC today).

The 1990s – a new confidence

By the 1990s, the world was changing: the spread of new forms of information technology and the development of vast multinational firms were bringing 'globalisation'. At the same time the collapse of communism in Russia and Eastern Europe had opened the way for the return of old ethnic and religious conflicts.

The Harare Commonwealth Declaration, 1991

The heads of government confirmed their commitment to the principles set out at Singapore in 1971.

They also pledged to work 'with renewed vigour' concentrating particularly on the following areas:

• the protection and promotion of the fundamental values of the Commonwealth:
- democracy
- democratic processes and institutions which reflect national circumstances
- the rule of law and the independence of the judiciary
- just and honest government
- fundamental human rights, including equal rights and opportunities for all citizens regardless of race, colour, creed or political belief
• equality for women
• universal access to education for the population of Commonwealth countries
• the promotion of sustainable development and the alleviation of poverty in the countries of the Commonwealth
• extending the benefits of development within a framework of human rights
• help for small Commonwealth states in tackling their particular economic and security problems

In the Commonwealth there was a new confidence. When the heads of government met in Harare, in Zimbabwe, in 1991, they issued a new Declaration. The Secretary-General called it 'our guide and beacon for the new century'.

Millbrook Plan of Action

Would the Harare Declaration really make a difference? In 1995, in New Zealand, the heads of government adopted a plan of action, to make sure that the principles of the association would be maintained by all members. One of the important features of this plan was the setting up of the Commonwealth Ministerial Action Group. This group was made up of eight foreign ministers. Its job was to meet to discuss what should be done if any Commonwealth country did not keep to the Harare principles. This Group was responsible for the decisions to suspend Pakistan (1999) and Fiji (2000, lifted 2001) from the Commonwealth after the overthrow in both countries of democratically elected governments. A special group of three heads of government recommended similar suspension of Zimbabwe (2002, and still suspended at the time of writing).

New members

The Commonwealth was given a tremendous boost by the return of South Africa in 1994. The fact that three other African countries asked to join the Commonwealth in the 1990s shows how respected the association was. These were:

• Namibia – for many years this country had been ruled as South West Africa by South Africa
• Cameroon – part of this country had been run by Britain, but it had been mostly a French colony
• Mozambique – this country had been a Portuguese colony, with no previous connection to Britain but it had played a vital role in the struggle for freedom in Zimbabwe and shared its borders with six Commonwealth countries.

Values of the Commonwealth

The values of this remarkable association are 'the glue' that binds the modern Commonwealth together.

Democracy All adult citizens should be able to choose who represents them in parliament and local councils by voting at elections.

Good governance Governments should conduct their business in an open way, so that everyone knows what is going on. They should always remember that they depend on the people for their power.

International co-operation Sharing problems and experiences can help countries to learn from each other.

Rule of law Even heads of government have to obey national and international law.

Consensus-building Talking about problems and working towards agreement is much better than confrontation.

Human rights It doesn't matter what gender, age, race, colour a person is, everyone has rights which should be respected.

Peace and order Wars between or within countries have terrible effects on people. It is only when there is peace that people can improve their lives.

Sustainable development It is important to try to improve people's lives, but this should not be at the cost of destroying the resources that future generations will need.

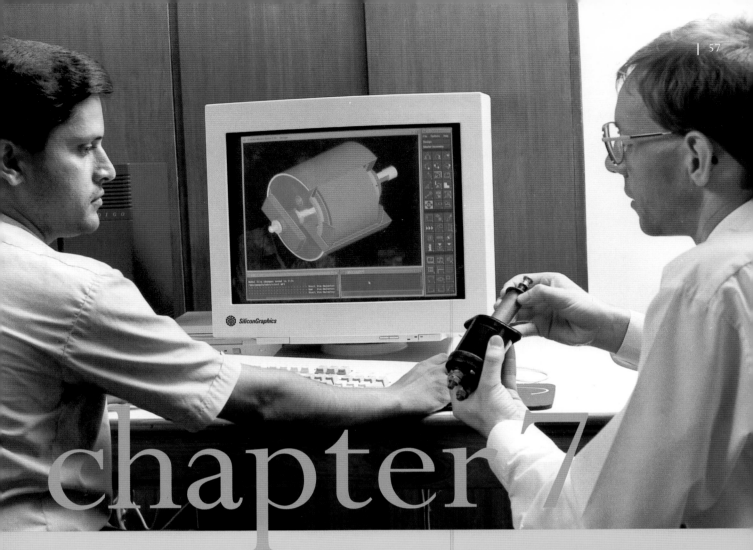

chapter 7

what does the Commonwealth do?

What does the modern Commonwealth actually do? This and the following chapter set out to answer this question. The current chapter describes some of the association's most people-centred activities, and Chapter 8 investigates what the Commonwealth does with and for young people. There is much that the Commonwealth does which cannot be included here – to describe everything would make this book far too long. You will not find mention in these chapters, for example, of the Commonwealth's work in reforming public service, in fighting corruption, in assisting developing countries to manage their debts, in strengthening the rule of law, in making trade fairer, or in developing systems for better financial management. To find out more about any of these and other Commonwealth activities see the list of useful addresses and websites on page 111.

Resolving conflicts and rebuilding societies

In 1990, Chief Emeka Anyaoku became Secretary-General of the Commonwealth.

'I spoke about a Commonwealth that would be seen to be guided in its existence and its actions by its principles. In other words, I made it quite clear that the time was past when the Commonwealth advocated such principles as democracy and human rights but didn't do much about them'.

Causes of conflict

The Commonwealth tries to resolve disputes and conflicts within and between its members as soon as possible. However, it is a basic belief of the modern Commonwealth that the causes of conflict are deeply-rooted. This is why the Commonwealth believes:

- that the principles of democracy and human rights are of fundamental importance
- that every person in the Commonwealth is entitled to a decent way of life, free from fear, hunger and disease

Commonwealth as peacemaker

It sometimes happens that a member country seeks help from the Commonwealth Secretary-General in solving a dispute. Why do they do that? It is because the Commonwealth is seen as a friendly, non-threatening organisation. It has credibility and can call on very experienced people to help solve problems.

If there is trouble in a country, the Secretary-General often visits the country himself, or he sends an envoy from another Commonwealth country. The main aim is to persuade the two sides in the dispute to talk to each other and solve their problems, before open conflict breaks out. In recent years, Commonwealth action has helped to solve disputes in Antigua and Barbuda, Lesotho, Mozambique, Papua New Guinea, Solomon Islands and Tanzania.

When violent conflict breaks out, then the Commonwealth Ministerial Action Group (CMAG) meets. This group is made up of eight Commonwealth foreign ministers. They decide what should be done.

Reconstruction in Sierra Leone

Low-cost housing project using local materials

There was a terrible civil war in the West African country of Sierra Leone during the 1990s. For ten years, men, women and children there suffered at the hands of violent, often drug-crazed soldiers. In this kind of war, it is civilians who are the victims – they are no longer safe on the street, in their villages, or even in their homes.

Now the war is over the people of Sierra Leone are trying to recover – a heartbreaking task when ten years of war have caused enormous suffering and death, when men and women have endured torture, rape and mutilation, when homes, whole communities, schools and clinics have been destroyed.

Women and children are very vulnerable in this kind of war. This girl was ten years old when she was captured by rebel soldiers.

'It was still dark in the morning. They raided our compound and put everybody in the house at gunpoint. I was taken away with my two brothers who were the same age. Mohamed, Alusine and myself were forced to carry ammunition and looted property on our heads to Kabala. It was so heavy, whenever we slowed our pace we were beaten with gun butts. On reaching Kabala one rebel deflowered me that very night – he was rough. He hurt me, and when I tried to fight he slapped me on my mouth, so that I couldn't

shout. Myself and my brother were drugged every morning. We used to take it as our breakfast. We were also trained to use guns: we used to go on raids every month.'

The Commonwealth played an active role in the attempts to bring peace to this troubled country. But conflict resolution is not just about making the peace – it is also about rebuilding societies to make sure the conflict does not return.

The Commonwealth is helping the reconstruction of Sierra Leone in various ways. One way is by reducing insecurity in the country by retraining the police force through a Commonwealth Police Development Task Force.

Another is by helping to ensure that women and young people are fully included in the discussions about the country's future. A big effort is being made to involve women in all levels of decision-making – only then will the issues which matter particularly to women – education, health care, housing, sanitation, agriculture – become priorities. And these issues are the key to the future of the country.

Encouraging democracy

The Harare Declaration states:
'We believe in the liberty of the individual under the law, in equal rights for all citizens regardless of gender, race, colour, creed or political belief, and in the individual's inalienable right to participate by means of free and democratic political processes in framing the society in which he or she lives'.

What makes a democracy?

In a democratic country citizens are aware of their rights and how to protect them. In a democracy there should also be:

- freedom of expression – people can voice their opinions freely, and the press is free to examine the actions of the country's leaders

- freedom of assembly – people can attend meetings and take part in peaceful protests

- independent judges who uphold the rule of law

Elections

The most obvious sign of a democracy is regular elections. This is when the people can choose who should represent them in local councils, or national government. The right to vote is one of the most precious rights we hold.

But elections can be conducted in a way which makes the result undemocratic. For example, electoral boundaries can be drawn up to favour a particular area or ethnic group, people can interfere with the ballot boxes, or people can try to vote more than once.

Commonwealth observer missions

For these reasons, there is a long history of sending Commonwealth citizens to observe elections in other countries. These observers watch every aspect of how the election is conducted, and write a report to say whether they think it has been fair and free. Over the last 12 years, observer missions have been sent to 25 Commonwealth countries.

Building a civil society

Democracy isn't just about having elections. It is also about having an open, just and honest government, about respect for the law and for the human rights of all people, including women, young people, people with disabilities and ethnic minorities.

Commonwealth observers at work

Being an election observer

Cheryl Dorall, who has been on many Commonwealth observer missions, describes what the observers do: 'Commonwealth observers often live and work in fairly rough places. They may be posted to small towns or villages in remote places up rivers, in jungles or by beaches. They travel by car, truck, small planes or boats to wherever polling stations are located. All the time they speak to ordinary people, election officials, security officers, journalists, women's groups and political parties to gauge how well the elections are being organised in their area and whether people will be able to vote freely.'

The Commonwealth Secretary-General carefully chooses each observer group from skilled and experienced politicians, lawyers, electoral officials, members of non-governmental organisations or journalists. They come from all over the Commonwealth, bringing with them different experiences in elections and electoral systems. The group is balanced between men and women. Very often, a former head of government chairs the group which can be very small (seven in Seychelles in 1993) or much larger (60 in South Africa in 1994).

For two weeks or so, Commonwealth election observers stay in a country to assess and analyse all aspects of the elections. On election day, they visit as many polling stations as they can. They consider whether electoral officials are efficient, and whether voters' names are on the register, whether the ballot is secret, if there is any fraud or whether voters are being threatened. At close of the poll they observe whether the ballot papers are counted properly and whether the results are communicated accurately and speedily.

After the count, the group meets up again. They discuss the electoral laws and regulations, the efficiency of the election organisers, whether all parties were able to campaign freely and fairly, the effectiveness of educating people on how and where to vote, the fairness of the elections and ballot counting. Based on this, they decide whether the elections as a whole were conducted fairly and whether people were able to vote freely for the representatives of their choice. Sometimes, they may make recommendations for change in laws or election systems.

Commonwealth observers are welcomed as independent assessors of elections and their recommendations are often accepted in order to strengthen democracy.'

To achieve this kind of society, ordinary people have to play an active part and governments have to listen to them. People cannot sit passively waiting for government to solve all their problems. When people take action, whether individually or in a group, they are building a civil society. A strong civil society is essential for embedding democracy into the very fabric of a country.

In 1997, the Commonwealth Foundation launched a project to investigate the nature of civil society in the Commonwealth – 47 countries were included. Ordinary citizens in these countries were asked to express their views on what makes a good society, and to suggest the roles that citizens and governments should play to achieve such a society. In 1999, the findings of the survey were published in *Citizens and Governance*, a report on civil society.

A South Pacific community meeting to discuss common problems

'A good society upholds the rule of law and human rights for all its people.' Zimbabwe

'A good society is one that makes laws to protect everybody ... a society where everybody – the poor, the middle class and the rich – get the same rights.' Jamaica

'A good society is one that's fair to all groups, where there is tolerance for all races.' Guyana

The project concluded that a strong civil society could be defined as one where citizens:

- are aware and informed

- understand their rights and responsibilities

- behave as active citizens in the family and community

- show solidarity, generosity and mutual support towards fellow citizens

- participate in local associations and organisations

- demonstrate assertive, caring and ethical leadership

- are enabled and encouraged to engage and connect with public institutions, officials and leaders on public concerns

- are not passive, apathetic or self-centred

The closing words of *Citizens and Governance* are: 'There is the need for all parties to act with faith and vision, courage and compassion. Travelling together in concert is the challenge. The journey to create a good society throughout the Commonwealth must now begin.'

You will find some examples of active citizenship in Chapter 9.

'What is the greatest thing in this world, I tell you; it is people, it is people, it is people.'

(Maori proverb)

Protecting human rights
The Commonwealth commitment

Each individual man, woman and child has rights. Protecting these rights is of great importance in the Commonwealth. The Harare Declaration, signed by the Commonwealth Heads of Government in 1991, confirmed the association's commitment to the protection of 'fundamental human rights, including equal rights and opportunities for all citizens regardless of race, colour, creed or political belief'.

Commitment to the promotion and protection of human rights was endorsed at the CHOGMs in South Africa in 1999, and in Australia in 2002.

Commonwealth actions
'To remain credible, relevant and meaningful for its citizens in the 21st century, the Commonwealth's rhetoric must be translated into real action through a rights-based approach.' (Commonwealth People's Festival Communiqué, 2001)

Children

The rights of children are too often ignored in today's world. Many children are driven by poverty to earn money for their families – they receive pitiful wages for long hours of labour, and are often not able to go to school. To prevent exploitation of children and to promote their rights, the Commonwealth encourages all its members to implement the United Nations Convention on the Rights of the Child.

It has also drawn up a curriculum on human rights and a teacher's guide, which can be adapted for use in member countries.

Commonwealth Human Rights Initiative (CHRI)

CHRI is an independent non-governmental organisation which aims to raise awareness of human rights in the Commonwealth. It does this, for example, by making sure that people know their rights to information, by encouraging police forces to be more accountable, by recognising the rights of prisoners, by encouraging public debate on issues to do with democracy and by persuading member countries to set up Human Rights Commissions.

Encouraging freedom of speech

One of the basic list of freedoms enshrined in the Universal Declaration of Human Rights is freedom of speech. People must be free to express their opinions and to criticise government actions. One way they do this is through the media. Newspapers, radio and television have a vital role to play in any democracy – they help to make the government accountable to its citizens. Throughout the Commonwealth there is a vigorous tradition of journalism and broadcasting – and the common use of English means there is ample opportunity for co-operation.

Organisations such as the Commonwealth Press Union, the Commonwealth Journalists' Association and the Commonwealth Broadcasting Association help to keep the standards high. They organise training courses and conferences where journalists and broadcasters from different countries can share experiences and discuss common problems.

Improving people's lives

The Commonwealth recognises:
'The importance and urgency of economic and social development to satisfy the basic needs and aspirations of the vast majority of the peoples of the world, and to seek the progressive removal of the wide disparities in living standards among our members.'

Poverty exists in every country – even the richest. Most of the members of the Commonwealth, however, are developing countries, where poverty is widespread. This doesn't mean that everyone in the country is poor. In every country there are people who have the opportunities to be successful – they receive a good education, they are healthy, they have access to modern technology, they have family support. These people can make choices about where they live and what they do. In

developed countries, such people make up a high proportion of the population; in developing countries they are a minority.

In developing countries many people have no choices. Life for them is a matter of survival – of trying to grow or obtain enough food to eat, of collecting water and firewood, of fighting disease. They have few opportunities for education, especially if they are girls, and access to modern technology is a dream.

What can the Commonwealth do?

There are many international organisations which are committed to the fight against poverty. What can the Commonwealth do which is special?

The Commonwealth Fund for Technical Co-operation (CFTC)

The Commonwealth Fund for Technical

Contrasting living conditions in India

Co-operation was started in 1971. It is based in the Commonwealth Secretariat in London. It receives its money from voluntary contributions from member governments. This funding is not large. It is therefore very important that CFTC spends its money wisely.

The Commonwealth always works in an informal way, making the most of the common language, the shared experiences of its members. It works through forming partnerships – not telling governments what to do, but working with them. These methods of working are among the strengths of the CFTC. It is small enough to respond quickly, to be flexible. It is trusted – governments of developing countries know that CFTC will offer impartial and good advice. CFTC assistance takes three forms:

'How can you sleep easy at night when your neighbour is hungry?' (Nelson Mandela)

Training

Training courses are provided to meet the specific needs of a country or region. Regular courses are held at Commonwealth centres of excellence, for example, in Malta and Singapore, on priority issues. Training in information technology (IT) skills is given special emphasis – developing countries need to develop the expertise which will enable them to compete in a world dominated by the information revolution.

Experts

CFTC experts are people who have the right background to visit the country concerned and help the local people solve the problems. Most of the experts are from developing countries themselves – and as such they have first-hand experience of the problems. About 450 experts were assigned to projects during 1999-2001. Some projects were short-term; many involved up to two years' work in the country concerned.

Advice

The CFTC offers advice to member governments, particularly those of small states (see page 78). This often is to do with economic and legal matters, the management of debt, and

how to develop strategies for competing on the world market.

Here are some examples of CFTC's work:
- assisting small island states draw up their maritime boundaries (important for countries which depend on fishing)
- creating new business opportunities in small states in the South Pacific
- developing computer software which helps countries manage the payments of their debts
- assisting countries in West Africa to identify and use local materials for building houses, schools and clinics, thus also providing job opportunities
- providing training for fishing communities around Lake Victoria in East Africa, so that the best use is made of valuable natural resources
- providing information on potential markets for exports from developing countries, so that all member countries can benefit from globalisation
- assisting the small West African state of The Gambia to open its own university
- providing leadership training for nurses and midwives in Asia and the Pacific
- funding speech therapy training projects in various countries

A CFTC expert offers advice in Sri Lanka

Working for small businesses

In 1996, the Commonwealth Science Council ran a workshop in Guyana on the use of simple solar-powered dryers for drying fish. Such dryers had already proved useful in Uganda. There, two commercial firms, Tropical Wholefoods (from the UK) and Fruits of the Nile (from Uganda), had used them to produce dried fruit for export to the UK and Europe.

Gertrude Pierre's fish processing business

Gertrude Pierre, who lives near the capital of Guyana, Georgetown, runs her own fish processing business. She used to dry her fish in the sun – and struggled along at the mercy of the weather and local pests, including naughty children. The drying fish were constantly exposed to the elements, dust, birds and passers-by.

However, her business has now been transformed through a simple solar drying shed that she has constructed in her back yard. The shed is six metres long by four metres wide and two metres high. It is covered in special plastic that traps the sun's heat and dries up to 450 kilograms of fish, which she buys from local fishermen.

She explains: 'The sun doesn't hit the fish directly. The fish are protected from the weather, the birds, the animals, the children and the dust. The process has helped me offer a better, cleaner, healthier product'.

Gertrude's customers are pleased with the improved quality and the business is now making a healthy profit. She is considering expanding into the export market.

Making a difference

CSAP – Commonwealth Service Abroad Programme – is one of the Commonwealth's newest ventures. Embarking on its first projects in 2001, it is already establishing itself as a low cost but innovative and exciting way of providing help to small states and developing countries.

What makes a CSAP project? Its aims have to include:
- reducing poverty
- helping young people and/or women
- assisting in the delivery of education or health
- being environmentally sustainable
- helping people make incomes or become entrepreneurs

Each project has to help as many people as possible – it has to be 'mass impact'. It also has to be focused on people, not institutions. This emphasis gives CSAP a unique 'grass roots' approach. Its projects make an immediate difference to people's lives – they 'put a smile on their faces'.

A CSAP project puts together a team in the country concerned with a volunteer from another country. The volunteers are high achievers, are often young, and most come from developing countries. There have been almost exactly the same number of male and female volunteers.

CSAP is quickly gaining a reputation for itself. Since its launch it has received more than 130 project proposals.

Some completed CSAP projects
Skills gap in Dominica

On the island of Dominica, the government wanted to know why there were so many unemployed young people when employers were crying out for skilled workers. A survey was done to identify the skills gap of the young people, and to find out their attitudes to work. A typical CSAP feature of the project was that it was organised by young people – young professionals who had themselves originated from the Caribbean.

Designing websites in Grenada

How can small businesses in the Caribbean

compete in the global market place? One way is by being on the web. But designing eye-catching websites is a skilled business.

The CSAP ran a training programme – and now Grenada has a community of web-designers. A similar programme was run in Sri Lanka, and others are planned.

CSAP volunteers speak

Bill Fallis is from Canada. He works in community education in a college in Toronto. He was a CSAP volunteer in Jamaica and St Lucia. There he developed ways to deliver secondary education through computer nodes in such places as community centres, church halls and prisons. In this way young people who have missed out on their education, are given a second chance.

'My wife and I both love travelling to other countries and meeting people who live in situations different from our own. We both feel that one can grow in amazing ways through the exposure to other cultures. We felt we had some skills we could share with others.'

Nana Ama Amamoo is Director of the African Families Foundation. She was a CSAP volunteer in Zimbabwe.

'I travelled to Zimbabwe and worked with people from 30 organisations on how best to run day care centres for orphaned children. We looked at how adults can provide safe and healthy environments for orphaned children by giving them good food, love and care, and protecting them from disease and abuse. The training programme also included how to involve children in the planning of services in the day care centres. The CSAP programme is an excellent example of working with people to help themselves.'

Indrani Lutchman is a fisheries biologist who works in Barbados. As a CSAP volunteer in that country, she helped to organise an important regional environmental workshop. Later she was able to share the Caribbean experience at a workshop in the South Pacific.

'I feel I have made a contribution to nature conservation in the Caribbean and the South Pacific. In the Caribbean the workshop report is the most current update of protected areas in the region. In terms of the South Pacific, the sharing of experiences from another region provided a different perspective and I had many positive comments and contacts on follow-up ideas.'

The future?

Ideas are coming in thick and fast, often for highly innovative projects. Some major themes are emerging:

Connecting people at grass roots level

While there is a long history of co-operation between governments and non-governmental organisations in the Commonwealth, CSAP's work in enabling ordinary people to share their experiences is breaking new ground. One example of this is how people from Sri Lanka, Uganda and Fiji Islands are learning from each other's experiences. There has been conflict between ethnic groups in each of these three very different countries. Diverting the energies of young people away from violence and into money-making enterprise is an important way to maintain peace. The three countries are learning from each other as to how this can be done.

Building up a pride in one's culture

Globalisation may be spreading a universal culture across the world. But one reaction to this is the desire of many communities to rebuild their own cultural heritage in a way which fits modern living. For example, there are plans in Kenya and Uganda to use up-to-date design and fashion skills to make traditional garments attractive to fashion-conscious young people.

Working with young people

One example of how young people want to get involved in the issues that matter, is the interest of youth groups in Barbados, Kenya, Fiji Islands and the Cook Islands in developing their acting, singing and dancing skills. This is not so that they can make a career for themselves in show business but so that they can use street theatre to raise awareness of issues such as AIDS, drugs and domestic violence among their peers.

Striving for gender equality
Changing roles

Attitudes to the roles of men and women are changing in many countries. No longer is a woman's world expected to be limited by the home and family. Increasingly girls are going to school, and women are finding jobs outside the home. As women become more educated, they choose to have fewer children. So families are becoming smaller — the nuclear family of husband, wife and children becoming more common. Men are taking on more domestic and parenting responsibilities.

> 'I don't think this housewife thing works any more ... Both people should run a house. It is good when a woman can get out there and look for work and hold down a job because it helps a lot ... All two work together. Then come home and share the responsibility. They clean the house and look after the kids together. I think that is how it should be.'
> (Sean, 20-year-old man, Barbados)

> 'Family lifestyle in the Solomons is gradually changing. In the past we live in communities and all we owned is for the community or extended family. However this is changing with the introduction of cash economy. Parents tend to care for their own nuclear family and not the extended family.'
> (Joan, elderly woman, Solomon Islands)

However, there are countries where attitudes are changing only slowly. In countries where most people live and work in the rural areas, the old extended family structures remain intact. The men bring home the money, maintain the homestead, and have authority over the family. The women grow food for the family, do the cleaning, the cooking, the laundry and often take on all aspects of parenting, including looking after sick children and making sure the children go to school. Often the female responsibilities include fetching water several times a day, and collecting firewood. These women may have very few rights — they may not be able to own property, for example, or inherit their husband's possessions.

Women in positions of power

Even in countries where equality between the sexes is generally recognised, there are remarkably few women in positions of power.

A group of delegates at the Commonwealth Women
Parliamentarians' meeting

At the time of writing, there are four
Commonwealth countries where over 30% of
the seats in parliament are held by women.
They are New Zealand, Mozambique, Uganda
and South Africa. There are another five
countries where female representation is over
20%. Over the whole Commonwealth, however,
the percentage is only 12.6. There is a
Commonwealth commitment to reach 30%
female representation in parliaments by 2005.

Commonwealth Plan of Action

The Commonwealth strives towards a world
where '…women and men have equal rights
and opportunities in all stages of their lives to
express their creativity in all fields of human
endeavour, and in which women are respected
and valued as equal and able partners in
establishing the values of social justice, equity,
democracy and respect for human rights'.
(Commonwealth Plan of Action on Gender
and Development, 1995)

Gender equality is not just about improving
the status of women. It is about treating women
and men equally. Gender equality is central to
the human rights agenda of the Commonwealth
and is enshrined in the Harare Declaration of
1991, which declares the Commonwealth's
commitment to the principle of 'equality
between men and women'.

Every Commonwealth programme, whether it
is to provide distance learning in Jamaica,
provide credit for young people in India, or
promote street theatre in Kenya, has to satisfy
the requirements – it has to promote gender
equality. In societies where women are treated
as inferiors, these programmes may have a
special emphasis on empowering women –
so that they can then have the same legal,
economic and social status as men.

Gender mainstreaming

The Commonwealth has been encouraging
member countries to introduce gender
mainstreaming. What this means is that

governments take gender issues into account in all planning and decision-making. Particularly important areas are finance, development planning and dealing with HIV/AIDS. Guidelines have been developed by the Gender Section of the Commonwealth Secretariat to help member governments do this.

Action against domestic violence

Domestic violence against women is a growing problem in many Commonwealth countries. The Commonwealth helps member countries develop national plans of action to deal with the problem.

Women's rights

The Commonwealth encourages all its members to ratify the Convention on the Elimination of All Forms of Discrimination against Women. This was proposed by the United Nations in 1979, and upholds the rights of women both within the family and outside. It has been ratified by 139 countries.

Women and post-conflict reconstruction

One of the most important activities of the Gender Section of the Commonwealth Secretariat has been its involvement in the reconstruction of the war-torn country of Sierra Leone, in West Africa. One of the poorest countries in the world, women had very few rights in pre-war Sierra Leone. Women and girls suffered terribly during the war, experiencing rape, torture, mutilation and the spread of HIV/AIDS and other sexually transmitted diseases. Women and children were also particularly affected by the destruction of agriculture, schools, clinics, water supplies and homes.

In 2000, the Commonwealth Secretariat organised a national consultation in Freetown, the capital of Sierra Leone. Two hundred and fifty women, men and young people discussed the ways in which the war had affected men, women, girls and boys, and how best to incorporate gender equality into all aspects of reconstruction.

'A genuine partnership between men and women in the struggle to build democracy and peace is bound to be a highly productive strategy. The partnership must have a sense of equality and of the indispensability of each person's contribution. It has no place for the traditional notion of the weaker sex associated with women, but certainly a huge place for brains, skills, determination and vision – all of which women possess no less.' (Joe Pemagbi, Chairman, National Commission for Democracy and Human Rights, Sierra Leone)

Young policewoman, Sierra Leone

Young women in enterprise

Employment opportunities for young women are often more limited than those for young men. One solution to this is for young women to start their own businesses, either individually or as a group. There are a lot of things which need to be thought about when setting up a business. The Commonwealth Youth Programme developed a workbook to help young women step their way through the process.

Giving everyone a chance

'Education empowers the poor, safeguards the vulnerable and promotes economic growth and social justice.' (Halifax Statement on Education, Conference of Commonwealth Education Ministers, 2000)

There are more than 135 million children in the world today who do not stand a chance. This is because they aren't able to go to primary school. Girls are often kept at home to help with younger children or do the housework. A lot of children have to earn money for their families. In Africa, many children have to stay at home to look after parents who have HIV/AIDS.

For those children who are lucky enough to go to school, the experience is sometimes unrewarding. There may be no learning materials, no books, no library – the teacher is quite likely to be untrained. Many children drop out before they finish primary school.

Getting more children into school

The Commonwealth has promised that by 2015 all children will have access to free primary education of good quality.

The Commonwealth is helping achieve this goal by:
- offering advice on how to teach different age levels in one class so that there can be a school even where there are not many people
- encouraging double shifts in primary schools, so that children either go to school in the morning or the afternoon
- promoting less formal, alternative methods of education for disadvantaged children

Improving the quality of education

The Commonwealth is helping to do this by:
- introducing citizenship education into school curricula
- improving curriculum and teaching styles in science and maths
- providing support for teachers
- producing multimedia learning materials for science and maths
- improving education programmes in small states
- helping families to keep girls in school until they have finished primary schooling

The problems do not end with primary schools. The numbers of children who go on to secondary education in developing countries are low, with tiny numbers going on to tertiary education. And there are over one billion adults who cannot read or write in the world.

Distance education and open learning

One of the most important ways in which the Commonwealth is helping give everyone a chance is through distance education and open learning.

The idea of distance education has been around for a long time. It means what it says – teacher and student don't meet in a classroom. Instead they communicate over a distance.

In the outback of Australia, children have been taught by distance education for many years. They live too far away to go to school each day. Instead, they learn at home, using two-way radios to talk to their teachers.

What is open learning? This is providing learning materials which anyone can use. There are Open Universities now in many countries which offer distance learning programmes even for those who did not finish secondary school.

Today, there are computers everywhere. People in all parts of the world send e-mails to each other and use the Internet. Video conferences make it possible for the student to see their teacher. The new information and communications technologies have transformed distance education.

Commonwealth of Learning (COL)

This Commonwealth organisation started work in 1989. It is based in Vancouver, Canada. Its work is to support open and distance learning systems, especially using new information and communications technologies (ICTs).

This organisation works in a typical Commonwealth way – in partnership with Commonwealth governments and institutions, and in co-operation with other organisations.

This diagram gives you some idea of the range of COL's activities:

Caribbean
COL has always worked closely with the University of the West Indies and is also:

• helping Caribbean students study 'at a distance' with Canadian universities

• helping to provide teacher education

• advising on using open schooling in Jamaica

• helping to organise a national conference on distance education in Guyana

COL is also investigating the possibility of establishing a virtual university to serve small Commonwealth states, most of which are located in the Pacific and Caribbean.

Asia

- using ICT to improve reading skills of adults in India

- establishing database of over 10,000 educational radio and television programmes in New Delhi

- implementing audio conferencing systems at Open Universities in India and Bangladesh

- developing courses for rural farmers in Bangladesh

- planning training courses for young people in rural areas in production of vegetables and fruit

- providing illiterate businesswomen of Bangladesh with business skills

Africa

- upgrading teachers of science, maths and technology in eight Southern and Eastern African countries

- upgrading teachers in Malawi who do not have qualifications

- producing high quality learning materials for junior secondary students in Southern and Eastern Africa

- using ICT to improve reading skills of adults in Zambia

- providing portable 'suitcase' radio broadcasting systems for rural communities

Pacific

COL has always worked closely with the University of the South Pacific and is also:

- developing learning materials in tourism, ICT and basic trade skills

- providing desk-top video editing systems to help produce educational videos

- co-ordinating efforts to establish electronic networking of schools

- facilitating a Pacific-wide technical skills training programme

- developing systems to provide a high school education to street children and out-of-school youth

Commonwealth co-operation in higher education

University education is a key factor in any country's development – graduates take up the top positions in government, the professions and business. Enabling students to study in another Commonwealth country for all or part of their courses can provide a fantastic opportunity for acquiring knowledge and for intellectual growth. It also means that friendships are formed which strengthen and extend Commonwealth understanding and co-operation when graduates return home and take up top positions.

The Commonwealth has a long tradition of co-operation at university level.

Nearly 500 universities belong to the Association of Commonwealth Universities (ACU). A person wanting to study in another country can use the ACU Yearbook or website to find out about courses offered. For 40 years, the Commonwealth Scholarship and Fellowship Plan (CSFP) has been providing the funds to make study abroad possible. More than 21,000 people have benefited from Commonwealth scholarships – they include a Prime Minister, many Cabinet Ministers and hundreds of senior figures in business and the professions. Students receiving these scholarships come from all Commonwealth countries – and the institutions at which they study can be found in over 20 countries, both developed and developing.

Rewarding talent

The important place of arts and culture in Commonwealth countries is recognised through a series of awards. These are organised by the Commonwealth Foundation.

Commonwealth Writers Prize

Some of the world's top writers live in the Commonwealth. The yearly writers prize, awarded for the best work of fiction, is thus an important event in the literary calendar. Winners receive £10,000. A best first book is also awarded, worth £3,000.

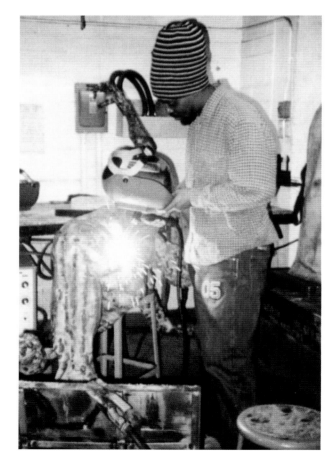

In 2003 the prize for the Best Book category went to *The Polished Hoe* by Austin Clarke from Canada; that for the Best First Book went to Sarah Hall of the UK for *Haweswater*. Prizewinners in 2002 came from Australia and South Africa.

> *'Perhaps literature illustrates best the unity in diversity which is so important a feature of our Commonwealth. Using the same English language, writers of many different races and backgrounds have enriched it with their individual qualities, and have expressed both universal human themes and the character of their own countries.'* (The Queen's Commonwealth Day message, 1974)

Commonwealth Arts and Crafts Awards

Ten young artists and craftspeople from Commonwealth countries receive this award every two years. With £6,000 it enables them to travel and study in another Commonwealth country.

Moutshi Banerjee is a printmaker in India. Her award enabled her to learn new printmaking techniques in the UK (see left).

Harry Mutasa is a sculptor from Zimbabwe. He was able to develop his skills in Canada (see left).

Commonwealth Short Story Competition

This competition is for short story writing for radio.

Arts and Culture Responsive Grants

Occasionally, the Commonwealth Foundation helps young artists from Commonwealth developing countries to travel to another country to participate in cultural events.

Commonwealth Photographic Awards

This annual competition is open to amateur and professional photographers. The photographs to the right show two prize-winning entries.

Fighting against HIV/AIDS

The overwhelming health issue for the Commonwealth is the HIV/AIDS pandemic.

HIV/AIDS – facts and figures

HIV/AIDS was first identified in early 1980s
Number of people identified with virus since then: 40 million
Number of people infected each day: 16,000
Number of deaths: more than 11 million

Effects on the Commonwealth

The nine most heavily affected countries are in the Commonwealth. They are in Sub-Saharan Africa. In some of these countries 30% of the people are infected with the virus. The effects are catastrophic:

- the disease has cut as much as 26 years from average life expectancy in some countries

- over 30% of children born to HIV-infected mothers, are themselves infected
- AIDS kills men and women in the prime of their working lives
- there are millions of orphans whose parents have died of HIV/AIDS

HIV/AIDS is not just a health issue. It has become a development crisis. At their meeting in Durban in 1999, the Commonwealth Heads of Government declared HIV/AIDS a Commonwealth emergency.

Commonwealth actions

The Commonwealth Secretary-General takes every opportunity to speak out about the devastating effects of HIV/AIDS, and urges the international community to give assistance to the countries most affected.

The Commonwealth Secretariat makes sure that examples of good practice in the care and support of men and women affected by HIV/AIDS are shared between affected countries. Girls and women are particularly badly affected

Ambassadors for Positive Living

Commonwealth programmes target young men and women – it is often these young people who become infected by HIV/AIDS. A successful example of how young people can help each other is Ambassadors for Positive Living.

Ambassadors for Positive Living is a programme which was started in Zambia, one of the African countries worst affected by HIV/AIDS. Instead of living in fear and isolation, this programme encourages young people who are HIV positive, to take control of their lives. There are 30 ambassadors in Zambia – all of them are HIV positive. They are prepared to talk about the disease they carry. They talk about it in schools, in clinics, in markets, even in the bars. They take part in radio and television programmes. They attend international conferences. They have visited ten other African countries.

The Ambassadors tell people how they can change their behaviour to reduce the spread of HIV/AIDS.

They encourage young people who have the disease to learn skills so that they can support themselves, to keep themselves healthy, to share their experiences. They campaign to ensure that the human rights of such people are respected.

You will find the story of one Ambassador for Positive Living on page 89.

Ambassador for Positive Living: Grace Mfune of Zambia (on right)

by HIV/AIDS. Because of their inferior status they lack the knowledge and the confidence to protect themselves from the sexual behaviour which spreads the disease. The Commonwealth's work on gender equality seeks to correct this imbalance (see also page 70).

Conserving the environment
Destruction of the rainforests

The rainforests of the world are being destroyed. In many places this is because farmers are cutting down the trees. This is so that they can grow crops or raise cattle. In many other areas, big timber firms are cutting down trees at a rapid rate. They hope to make high profits from selling the valuable wood on world markets.

The effects of this are serious for the future of the planet. The loss of trees is helping to cause global warming. The burning of trees is causing widespread pollution. The people, animals and plants that live in the rainforests are losing their livelihood and their habitat. We are all losing valuable knowledge about the potential benefits of the rainforest plants.

Iwokrama – a place of refuge

But deep in the remote forests of the South American country of Guyana a unique experiment is taking place. At the meeting of Commonwealth Heads of Government in 1989,

the prime minister of Guyana, Desmond Hoyte, made the Commonwealth an offer. His government was prepared to set aside an area of rainforest covering nearly 4,000 square kilometres. What was proposed was new: one half of the area would remain as an untouched wilderness; the other half would be managed. The 'managed' half was to be run in such a way that the people, animals and plants benefit. What was being proposed was an experiment in sustainable development.

A management centre was set up in the capital of Guyana, Georgetown. The area of Iwokrama is a day's drive away in a four-wheel drive vehicle, and then by boat on the mighty River Essequibo.

There are several partners involved in the project:

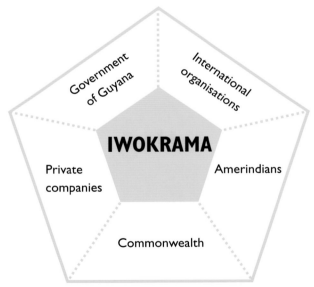

The key partners are the people who live in the forest – the Amerindians. It is vital to the project that they are treated with justice and respect. They have helped to build the field centre in Iwokrama; they provide knowledge on the valuable medicinal plants which can be found in the forest. They will benefit from employment provided by properly managed timber production, eco-tourism and the collection of medicinal plants.

Amerindian family

Working at Iwokrama

The experts who work at Iwokrama are recruited from other countries in the Commonwealth, often the developing ones.

In 2000 Francis Kahembwe, a forestry expert from Uganda, was recruited by CFTC to work at Iwokrama for two years. Part of his work was to zone the forest into the two parts, so that management plans can be developed. He has worked closely with the local communities to do that.

'I have spent time with the local communities living in and around Iwokrama forest and the indigenous knowledge these people have about the forest and its use is amazing. One of my tasks is to work with these communities to develop their ability to benefit from the Iwokrama forest and also together address the complex issues relating to sustainable development.'

Assisting small states

Of the 54 member countries of the Commonwealth, 32 are classified as small states. Most of these have a population of less than 1.5 million. Many are islands – in the Caribbean, the Pacific and the Indian Ocean. Because of the high number of such states in the Commonwealth, the association has developed a unique understanding of their problems.

Small states need particular assistance because:
• they are prone to natural disasters, such as hurricanes, flooding and tsunami

Hurricane damage, Western Samoa

• they tend to rely on one source of income, such as tourism, or the export of sugar or bananas
• they have a limited supply of talented people – many citizens move away from the small states to seek better opportunities elsewhere
• they are very dependent on trade with other countries – but it is difficult for small countries to compete in today's globalised market
• they are often remote, which means it costs a lot to transport goods to and fro

In all Commonwealth programmes, special account is taken of the needs of small states. A high proportion of CFTC projects (see page 64) provide assistance for small states.

chapter 8

the Commonwealth and young people

One-third of the world's young people (those aged between 15 and 29) live in the Commonwealth. They are the greatest resource for the future of Commonwealth countries.

'It is sometimes easy for those in authority to regard young people as "the problem". To do so is to ignore cause and effect. The real "problem" lies in the inability of society to respond to the needs and challenges of new generations of young people – especially those with different ethnic backgrounds, colour and/or culture.' (Commission for Racial Equality, 1980.)

The Commonwealth believes strongly that, rather than being regarded as a problem, young people should be empowered and given a voice.

The Commonwealth Youth Programme (CYP)

The CYP was formed in 1973 on the instructions of the Commonwealth Heads of Government. It began as a training and information programme for youth workers. Now it is a network based around Commonwealth youth ministries and is recognised as one of the world's leading agencies working with young people.

It has regional centres in Africa, Asia, the Caribbean and the South Pacific, and a pan-Commonwealth office in the Commonwealth Secretariat in London.

'Empowering young people means creating ... conditions under which young people can act on their own behalf, and on their own terms, rather than at the direction of others.' (The Commonwealth Plan of Action for Youth Empowerment to the Year 2005)

Listening to young people

'To young people I would say: Don't let life go by. Life is truly a game, and we all hold cards.' Edward Registe, Caribbean co-ordinator, Commonwealth Youth Caucus

'To young people, I'd use an African saying – Contribute your quarter.' Mulako Mwanamwalye, outgoing Chairperson, Commonwealth Youth Caucus

The Commonwealth has established a structure which encourages young people to participate in the discussions and decision-making of the association.

The Commonwealth Youth Caucus

The Youth Caucus leads a network of young people which spreads across all 54 countries of the Commonwealth. There are five members of this caucus. The Pan-Commonwealth Youth Representative, the Chairperson of the caucus, represents the caucus at meetings of the Commonwealth Youth Ministers where youth policy affecting the whole of the Commonwealth is discussed. She, or he, has four colleagues, who represent the regions of Africa, the Caribbean, Asia and the South Pacific.

The Pan-Commonwealth Youth Representative has full speaking rights at Commonwealth Youth Ministers Meetings, and also at planning meetings of the CYP.

The members of the caucus are elected by regional youth conferences which take place every three years. At these conferences, two representatives (one female, one male) from each country in the region gather to discuss matters of particular concern to young people. The national representatives in their turn are selected by their national governments.

What does the Youth Caucus do? These are the words of Mulako Mwanamwalye, out-going Chair:

'• we represent the views/opinion of young people on issues that directly or indirectly affect them
• we "youth proof" CYP programmes
• we engage in advocacy aimed at placing youth issues on the national agenda in Commonwealth countries
• we promote Commonwealth values among young people (who form more than 50% of the population in many developing member countries)
• we serve as a link between the Commonwealth Youth Programme and grass roots youth organisations
• we keep young people informed of CYP programmes'

Youth Caucus profile I

Vida Gorang comes from Ghana. When she was about 25 she was selected to be a youth representative for her region of Ghana on the National Youth Council of Ghana. (This council comprised two representatives from each of Ghana's ten regions.) After that she was chosen to represent her country at an African meeting for young people held in Tanzania. In 1997, she attended the Commonwealth Youth Forum which was held in Edinburgh, UK, and in 2000 she became the regional co-ordinator for Africa on the Commonwealth Youth Caucus.

Vida stresses the need for youth representatives to be able to motivate themselves, to know how to mobilise resources and to speak out. She points out that the Commonwealth has a superb structure in place to ensure that young people participate – it is up to the young people themselves as to how they can make a difference in people's lives at grass roots level.

'A society that cuts itself off from its youth severs its lifeline. But a society that engages their interest, enlists their talents and liberates their energies, brings hope to the entire world.'

(Kofi Annan, United Nations Secretary-General)

The Commonwealth Youth Forum

The first Commonwealth Youth Forum took place at the same time as the Commonwealth Heads of Government Meeting in Edinburgh in 1997, and the second took place in Durban in 1999. In 2001 the third youth forum was hosted by the Government of Australia – it was attended by 29 Australian delegates and one male and one female delegate from 51 Commonwealth countries.

The youth forums are intended to encourage the young people of the Commonwealth:
* to identify their vision for the Commonwealth in the 21st century
* to address issues of concern to young people
* to increase their knowledge and understanding of the Commonwealth
* to promote the outcomes of the forum on their return home

'It's not always the big guys who get the work done. It's those little people with a genuine interest in what they do ... with a domino effect we can reach many.'

(Representative at CitizenYou)

Youth Caucus profile 2

Damien Hughes comes from Anguilla in the Caribbean. With degrees in Political Science, Public Policy and Constitutional Law he also plays Davis Cup Tennis for the Eastern Caribbean. Damien is Chairman of the National Youth Policy Formulation Task Force in Anguilla and Secretary of the Anguilla National Youth Council. One of his main concerns is youth unemployment: in the Caribbean most countries have 40% unemployment among 15-19 year olds, and around 28% unemployment among 20-24 year olds.

'What a lot of us in National Youth Councils have been calling for is a Caribbean Youth Dialogue on Youth Employment ... Among the objectives would be to:

* establish and support the work of youth employment networks
* lobby for national youth policies, national action plans for youth employment, national youth employment funds...
* harness the media to create public awareness and place the burning issue of youth unemployment on the global agenda
* foster friendships, and the exchange of information, cultural knowledge and understanding'

(from 'Employment is the Key' by Damien Hughes, *C21: Young People in a Changing Commonwealth*, 2002)

CitizenYou

In 2002, the Youth Exchange Council took the lead in organising a massive young people's conference in Sunderland, UK. It was timed to coincide with both the Queen's Golden Jubilee as Head of the Commonwealth and the Commonwealth Games.

Around 60 young men and women from the UK acted as hosts for young people from over 50 Commonwealth countries. At this week-long Commonwealth Youth Summit, around 250 young people came together to share their vision of active citizenship.

'Close your eyes. Think of all the negative perceptions of young people you have. See that big green garbage can on your left? Take 'em and dump 'em'.

(Ifasina, from Belize at CitizenYou)

'Young people are vital to the processes of development, democracy and participation. We, as citizens of the Commonwealth, have the responsibility, as well as the right, to participate in making change'.

The participants at CitizenYou made this declaration:

Vision

Many visions of the good society are available to us. A true democracy includes, but goes far beyond, free and fair elections. It thrives upon the mutual influence of actors at all levels, from committed individuals, to families and communities, to non-governmental organisations, to accountable, transparent government.

- At national level, it means that one class, culture, caste, religion, sex or race does not dominate another.
- At international level, it means that people's governments are not dictated to by more powerful forces.

These outcomes are only possible by permitting and encouraging citizen participation, especially that of young people. Young people must be assured of a future free of poverty, HIV/AIDS and environmental degradation.

Recommendations

1 The Commonwealth represents nearly two billion people, the majority of them living in poverty, not a periodic meeting of officials and heads of state. It must engage with its peoples and their priorities: HIV/AIDS; employment; education. Developed Commonwealth member countries must do more to relieve the debt burden of developing member countries.

2 Commonwealth governments must honour their commitments to:
- human rights
- overseas development assistance targets
- youth empowerment
- good governance – including the establishment of independent youth organisations

3 Citizenship education is a broad process that cannot be limited to the formal education system. Families, communities and young people must all play a role. Formal citizenship education should be concerned with political facts, not political values. Our political values should emerge from open dialogue between us all. This was our experience at CitizenYou.

4 The Commonwealth must start focusing on the implementation and communication of policies that are currently sitting on the shelf. We are not aware of what the Commonwealth is doing with young people or HIV/AIDS. We need better monitoring and evaluation of all development work, and this should involve young people.

5 We feel privileged to have participated in CitizenYou. We are determined to share our learning back in our home countries. There should be continuity between Commonwealth youth conferences to keep the momentum. The next Commonwealth youth conference should take HIV/AIDS as its theme. HIV/AIDS is the greatest threat we face.

Youth parliaments

It is one thing to give young people a voice in their own meetings and conferences – but can they really affect what their national governments do? The whole democratic process of elections, political parties, parliamentary procedures and debates can be a real turn-off for young people. There are many countries in the Commonwealth where the turnout of young people at general elections is very low. One way to tackle this is to promote a better understanding of the democratic system among young people – and one way of doing that is to hold youth parliaments.

Some Commonwealth countries have been holding youth parliaments for many years – for example, Norfolk Island (a tiny territory governed by Australia, which has just 2,000 people), Jersey (Channel Islands) and the Canadian province of Alberta. Two regional youth parliaments have been held in the Caribbean.

The Commonwealth Parliamentary Association (CPA) has organised two pan-Commonwealth

Youth Parliaments, in 1997 and 2000. The Millennium Youth Parliament of 2000 involved over 100 young people coming from all the Commonwealth regions. This was what was said by two of those who participated:

'I would be very keen to help in the establishment of a Scottish Youth Parliament ... the standard of this event was much higher than anything I had been involved with before. Debates were fast-flowing, witty and had a sense of reality. They tended to stay focused and serious issues were discussed.' (James North, Scotland)

'The CPA should encourage every region ... to hold Youth Parliaments ... This move will encourage the youth to get instructed in parliamentary business and politics and hence curb the problem of low voter turnout among the young people.' (Rehema Kabiru, Kenya)

The Millennium Youth Parliament 2000

Stories from the South Pacific

One of the things the Commonwealth can do for young people is to open up opportunities. If young people have talent and energy, and show a commitment to improving the life of young people in their countries, the Commonwealth can provide a focus for their energies, a way in which they can make a real difference.

These four young people all live in the South Pacific. They are aged from 18 to 29. Coming from very different backgrounds, they share a common motivation – to change the world for the better.

Sen Thong is of Cambodian background and lives in Wellington, in Aotearea/New Zealand. He was brought up in the inner city: 'Unfortunately this involved being brats in the way of crime, substance experimentation, truancy and other anti-social actions.'

Music was always an integral part of Sen's life. 'When I was 15, I discovered Hip Hop culture. Growing up in an urban environment I was always exposed to rap, electronic, rock and punk music. It was when I saw a movie that contained a DJ scratching his records that I was influenced to investigate this music form. What I discovered was a real culture, deeper than just rap music as we are exposed to through mass media and urban pop culture, but a global culture that combines music, dance, oral story telling, art and an emphasis on creativity. This culture is very similar to those of the Maori and Pacific Islanders, who did not use written methods to record history, but oral stories, art, song and dance. This I feel is one of the many strong reasons why Maori and Pacific Island youth have absorbed Hip Hop attitudes into their general way of life.'

Sen decided that he wanted to prove to society that city kids are potential citizens, not troublemakers. He worked hard, and took a Law degree. He established New Zealand's only Hip Hop magazine and started a charity to support youth arts and cultural initiatives. He also became a member of Wellington City Youth Council.

'Recently I was nominated to attend the Youth Employment Summit 2002 (YES2002) in Alexandria, Egypt. I was fortunate to attend as the only representative from New Zealand, the result of a strong funding campaign. As my first major trip abroad and first international conference, I was unprepared for what YES2002 would offer. I was amazed at the representation of the world at this event, the opportunities to gain friendships and contacts with people globally and the knowledge that was provided on a subject of which, I had limited prior knowledge. On the conclusion of YES2002 I was inspired! My eyes and senses were awakened to the issues globally concerning youth employment and in what capacity I could contribute to reducing these issues.'

Emele (Emily) Petelo is from the Kingdom of Tonga.

'Tongans are known amongst the Pacific Islands as born orators, comedians, poets and singers. I can guarantee that if you meet a group of laughing Pacific Islanders, a Tongan will be the centre of attention because they would either be telling a joke or fabricating a story or singing a song ... They possess the friendliest of manners, have an excellent sense of humour, extremely strong family ties, strongest of cultures and generally call themselves Christians.'

Emele started out representing young people at her church and became a board member of the Catholic National Youth Council. At the time of writing, she is National Co-ordinator for the National Youth Congress – and as such attended the Regional Youth Forum organised by the Commonwealth Youth Programme.

'When I started working with the National Youth Congress, I thought that I had it all. Boy! Have I ever

Kari Austin is a Maori from a small town in Aotearea/New Zealand: 'My culture, heritage, identity and language have always been very important to me.' Her family moved to the city of Christchurch when she was six and for a brief time at the school there she enjoyed an education steeped in Maori culture.

'We were all one big family. We did everything together, worked, played, sang, and did kapahaka (Maori cultural performing). The Maori kids also learnt some Samoan songs from the Samoan group that was at our school. All of our classes were in a mixture of both English and Maori. We learnt Maori songs, traditions, protocol, myths and legends, while also learning our other subjects such as maths, reading, spelling and writing. We had the best of both worlds and I was in my element.'

Later she moved back to a small town and went to a school where she and her brothers were the only Maori children.

'I was introduced to bullying and racist name calling for the first time in my life. It hurt me a lot, but I would just ignore it and go play footie with the boys.'

Kari went on to a Catholic secondary school: 'I was the only one of my Maori friends who went to a Catholic school, and one of the few who succeeded in my academic studies and who went right through to Year 13. I have no doubt that they had the ability, because they were all very clever kids. They just didn't. Because I didn't get into alcohol heavily, or into drugs and crime, and because I had goals for myself, and was committed to going to university, and making something of myself, I was labelled a "coconut" by some. Which is a term used for someone who is brown on the outside, but white on the inside.

Just as there is a negative attitude about youth as a whole, there is an even worse attitude about Maori youth. There are people like me, who know that that isn't how it is, and who go out to prove all of those people wrong, but there are so many more who just go along with it, and become just another stereotyped statistic ... of a school dropout, a teen pregnancy, a youth offender, a substance abuser, a benefit dependent ... the list goes on.

When I had the opportunity of being a part of the Commonwealth Youth Programme (CYP), and a Regional Youth Forum (RYF) Representative for New Zealand, I jumped at the chance. Because I recognised all the issues that not only Maori youth were faced with, but all youth collectively, and not only in New Zealand, or the South Pacific, but all over the Commonwealth and the world. And I wanted to be a part of that. I wanted to be a part of something that was so committed to working together, for the well-being of our young people.'

been so wrong! After calling myself a few choice names, I started gathering some few basic principles both in theories and practice. Working with foreign volunteers like the US Peace Corps, Australian Youth Ambassadors and Japanese Overseas Consultant Volunteers has really cleaned up my act. The layer of "innocent" has been pulled away and the stark reality allowed to penetrate the fog of the sheltered life I was used to. Here I was, I was lamenting about "being bored", having no privacy and feeling the guilt of the accusing looks when years passed and I remain as single as ever. I did not know that my fellow sisters and brothers out there are facing gigantic problems compared to my insignificant ones. Some are starving while I am throwing food away so my mother thinks I ate it (to keep my size 10 figure); they are facing drugs problems and abuses while I complain about not being allowed more freedom to stay out late more often; some are homeless while I am complaining about my house being too homely. In short, what I have considered a prison would be the sample of Heaven to some youth out there.'

Orisi Seru Qaranivalu is a pharmacist from Fiji Islands. In January 2002, he was able to buy his own business and thus became an entrepreneur.

'In May 2002 I was fortunate enough to be selected as a participant in the Commonwealth Youth Programme (CYP), Body Shop, and UNDP Young Entrepreneurs Retail Skills Training Workshop held in Suva. This workshop brought together 19 eager young entrepreneurs and proposed entrepreneurs. The enthusiasm and professionalism of the resource people at this workshop rubbed off on the participants and thus led to the creation of the Fiji Islands Young Entrepreneurs Association (FIYEA) (pronounced FIRE!) I was thrust into the leadership role of FIYEA.

The Ministry of Youth nominated FIYEA to represent the nation along with the Minister for Youth to the Youth Employment Summit (YES) 2002, in Alexandria, Egypt. The Commonwealth Youth Programme provided funding for the trip. I was forever grateful. The experience at YES2002 was overwhelming. It brought together young entrepreneurs from all over the globe, with their different scenarios, experiences, and ideas, which put together, was a treasure trove of practical innovations. The networks developed in Alexandria were invaluable and within four months of its creation FIYEA was part of the global network of entrepreneurs. I was now a global citizen.

Entrepreneurship, social responsibility, and global citizenship in nine months – nothing short of amazing!'

Commonwealth youth activities
Youth Credit Initiative

One way of empowering young people is to make it possible for them to start their own businesses. What stops many young people from doing this is the lack of money. When they go to banks for loans, they are told that their businesses are too small, or that they cannot be trusted to repay the money. The Youth Credit Initiative makes small sums of money (often starting out at between $50 and $100) available to young people, especially young women. It also provides training in marketing and management, and assistance in drawing up a business plan. The CYP piloted the Youth Credit Initiative in

Zambia, India, Guyana and Solomon Islands. They then developed a toolkit so that other countries could adapt the initiative for themselves.

Anita in India was able to start a laundry and ironing business which is now expanding. She said: 'My family is very proud of me. I have money over every week, after making the repayments.'

Youth in Development Diploma

The CYP began training youth workers in the 1970s. Its Youth in Development Diploma is centred on the Commonwealth values of equality, human rights and democracy. Diploma graduates have often risen to high posts in their

Youth Credit Initiative in St Vincent and the Grenadines

About half the adults in these Caribbean islands are unemployed and many of these are young people. Inspired by the Youth Credit Initiative, the National Commercial Bank set up a fund of half a million dollars, to provide small loans for people who wanted to set up businesses. Half of this money was for young women and men. The businesses that the money has helped to set up include:

- Hairdressers
- Grocery and convenience stores
- Crafts
- Making clothes
- Garden and home care
- Small manufacturing, for example herbal drinks, confectionery

I did not know that you can be so brave, my son ...

Mathew Mbiti was the Zambia co-ordinator for Young Ambassadors for Positive Living. This is his story.
'I was born on 29 September, 1975, the second of five children. My mother died in 1994 when I was writing my secondary school final examinations. She was the breadwinner of the family. My father was not working. There was no-one to pay for my further education. I raised money to continue school by selling second-hand clothes. Then I started running a bottle store and made a lot of money. I got involved with a girl whom I planned to marry, but later on she died. I didn't know what killed her.

In March 1998 I got sick. I was so thin and weighed 39 kilograms – barely more than half my normal weight. I went to the hospital, where they diagnosed tuberculosis. In our community, once one has TB, people conclude that it is AIDS. People were saying I had AIDS. The only way to prove them wrong was to take an HIV test.

When I went for the results I was told I was HIV positive. I started crying. I saw death two steps ahead. The counsellor told me: "Mathew! This is not the end of your life but the beginning of your new life". He told me to go to Hope House – a centre where HIV positive people are trained to live with the virus, and where I learnt new skills.

I didn't tell my family I was going to Hope House. I did not want anyone to know my HIV positive status.

I was persuaded by a friend to take part in an American television programme about AIDS. A Zambian television crew heard about this and asked if I would take part in a short programme called Health Beat. They said that very few people would see the programme.

One day, I came home from Hope House as usual. My family was watching TV in the living room. Suddenly I heard my young brother calling me in panic. I rushed into the room. My brother pointed to the television. It was me. Under the picture were the words "Mathew Mbiti – HIV positive".

I knew that everyone in the world had seen me. I felt humiliated and hated myself. I rushed to the bedroom and the first thing that came into my head was to commit suicide. Then I heard someone banging and pushing at the door. My father came in and said "I did not know you could be so brave, my son. Keep up the good work you have started. But you have to be strong with the community out there. Most people you think love you will now shun you".

For almost two weeks, I did not come out of the house. Then I saw a counsellor who encouraged me to continue sharing my experience. I moved out of my home and rented a room in another compound. I had nothing in the house apart from my clothes, one blanket, an electric plate and some plates for cooking. I gave my time to doing AIDS prevention work.

Now I am well recognised in my country. A lot of young people come to me for counselling. I have helped to break the stigma attached to HIV/AIDS.'

Mathew Mbiti passed away in 2002.

countries. In recent years, the techniques of distance education have been used to enable even more people to take the course.

Young people and HIV/AIDS

HIV/AIDS is a killer disease. Young men and women who become HIV positive also suffer discrimination in the workplace and are often made to feel ashamed. They often try to keep their condition secret. Many consider suicide.

You read about HIV/AIDS and the CYP programme – Ambassadors for Positive Living –

in Chapter 7 (see page 76). See the box above for one Ambassador's story.

Increasing understanding of the Commonwealth
Commonwealth Youth Exchange Council (CYEC)

This organisation was started 30 years ago to encourage exchanges between young people in the UK and other Commonwealth countries. CYEC promotes and supports links between young people in the UK and other countries across the Commonwealth – it is estimated that two-thirds of primary school children in Britain have a relative as close as or closer than second cousin in another Commonwealth country.

Most of the young people who take part are between 16 and 20. It is not just a matter of signing up for an exotic holiday in a distant land. Preparations for an exchange usually take two to three years, and the young people are actively involved in all the planning stages. The group discusses and agrees the theme of their visit – some themes of recent exchanges have been:

- comparing what it is like to live in an area of conflict (Belfast, Northern Ireland and Sri Lanka)
- finding out about a different culture (Islington, England and Jamaica)
- learning how cultural diversity affects religion (Cardiff, Wales and Kenya)
- learning about ways to combat poverty (Glasgow, Scotland and Bangladesh)
- working together to help the community (Tanzania and Cumbria, England)
- comparing what it is like to live on a small island (Shetland, Scotland and Trinidad and Tobago)

The exchange usually involves the young people staying with host families. This is how some of the young people who have participated in an exchange have described their experience:

'We have total difference in sense of humour from the people of Bangladesh, particularly the young people. We have different habits, different ways of communicating certain things, but fundamentally we understand each other's cultures.' (Bangladesh Youth League, Luton, England and an NGO in Bangladesh establishing literacy among rural peoples)

'I've learned that if we take the time to understand and learn more about each other, we find more similarities than differences. No matter how far round the world you go, you can always find people you can relate to.' (Shetland, Scotland and Trinidad and Tobago)

'What an experience – the whole event exceeded expectations in every way. We were all challenged in a variety of ways and overcame these together, growing in the process.' (Suffolk, England and Canada)

'This exchange has changed my lifestyle – I now make better use of my personal time in college and at work. It has made me realise that it IS possible to achieve what you want in life.' (Islington, England and Jamaica)

Youth for the future

In 2002, at the Heads of Government Meeting at Coolum, Australia, the Commonwealth made a commitment to its young people in the 'Youth for the Future' initiative. This is intended to encourage Commonwealth co-operation in youth enterprise development, youth volunteering, youth mentoring and youth leadership. Secretary-General Don McKinnon said: 'My single and most important message to young people and civil society is this: all Commonwealth member governments have agreed that young people should be at the core of our development agenda in order to sustain the future of the Commonwealth and its people'.

The Commonwealth has played an important role in the reconstruction of the West African country of Sierra Leone, after long years of civil war. During this war 80% of the schools were destroyed and HIV/AIDS exploded across the country. (For more information see Chapter 7, page 70.)

One of the speakers at a National Consultation on Women and Men in Partnership for Post-Conflict Reconstruction in Sierra Leone was **Steve Mokwena**, formerly Chief Executive Officer of the South African Youth Commission. He talked about the importance of involving young people in the reconstruction process. Among other things he said:

'In South Africa we assumed that because young people had been exposed to trauma and violence ... what we had to do was "fix" them ... With hindsight ... we learned that once you bring young people into the process of seeking solutions, and imagining and dreaming an alternative vision, the process itself has a healing, redemptive, restorative capacity.'

'I find that young people, when asked to do something or when given a chance to do something, they can actually do what needs to be done.'

chapter 9

being a Commonwealth citizen

We have looked at the Commonwealth as an organisation that carries out a range of official and non-official activities. **Now it is time to consider what it means to be an individual who is part of this family of nations.** Simply by living in one of the countries of the Commonwealth, we are Commonwealth citizens. This role could be viewed as a passive one, or instead, taken on in a thoughtful, responsible way, by becoming aware of both the duties and the rights involved. With this knowledge, Commonwealth citizens would then have the opportunity to participate meaningfully and effectively in the making of decisions that affect them, and play a part in activities that make a positive difference, locally, nationally and throughout the Commonwealth.

A responsible Commonwealth citizen is someone who:
- realises that everyone is entitled to the fundamental conditions necessary for freedom and well-being
- respects and values diversity
- is committed to making a difference in their own community
- is willing to work with others to make the world a fairer place and to protect its resources for future generations

Becoming informed Commonwealth citizens

In the 21st century, for some people, technological advances allow easy and rapid contact between Commonwealth nations across the world. Television, the Internet and the World Wide Web allow information to spread faster than ever before, bringing global ideas and concerns into our schools and homes, but it's important to remember that traditional forms of communication still have their place and can be essential to remote communities.

There has always been a gap between those people and communities who have access to

Did you know that Trevor Baylis (right) invented the clockwork radio after watching a TV programme about the spread of AIDS in Africa, and realising that there was a need for an educational tool that did not rely on electricity or batteries?

Did you know that villagers in rural southern India are getting their first taste of the Internet, via motorbike courier? Crop reports and health information are downloaded onto a laptop and taken to remote areas currently outside the country's communications infrastructure.

information technology and those who do not, but there are many signs that the developing world is catching up.

Improvements in communication allow us to be informed about the difficulties and the successes of other countries. We can speak out ourselves and learn from others. With our increased understanding, we have the information necessary to become committed and active citizens of the Commonwealth, harnessing the power of communication in a positive way.

Rights and responsibilities

Commonwealth heads of government have promised that they will keep to a set of principles that concentrate on:

- good governance, including democracy and the rule of law
- human rights, including equal rights
- protection of the environment through sustainable development

They also agree to abide by the Universal Declaration of Human Rights, and the special provisions for children, set out in the Convention on the Rights of the Child. We expect our governments to uphold our rights.

More than this, individual citizens of the Commonwealth have a responsibility too, to respect these rights and freedoms, and to stand up to people who take no notice of the agreed ways to behave towards others.

Everyone has civil and political rights, which deal with our entitlement not to be interfered with by the state or others, including the right to:

- life
- privacy
- freedom of movement
- hold religious or political beliefs
- protection from arbitrary arrest
- a fair trial

We also have economic, social and cultural rights that deal with our welfare and well-being, such as the right to:

- an adequate standard of living
- education
- health care
- reasonable working conditions

What can I do?

As a young individual, it is easy to think 'Nobody will listen to me. How can I make a difference in the world?' It is easy to imagine

Young children as learners and teachers

Shobu says: 'I will have less disease if I learn well. I already have changed some behaviour by wearing slippers to the latrine to protect me from getting worms in my feet. I didn't even know about washing my hands before but now I do. I tell my family and neighbours about hand washing and keeping things clean. Anyone I see using a bad hygiene practice I tell them. Initially my parents would tell me to shut up as I was just a child. But the group I'm with now would get together then go and tell these adults together about the good hygiene. We are braver in a group and feel like we can tell adults what to do more with that extra confidence.'

that it is only famous, powerful people who can bring about change. Here is a different view:

'Change comes from small initiatives which work; initiatives which, imitated, become the fashion. We cannot wait for great visions from great people for they are in short supply. It is up to us to light our own small fires in the darkness.'

(Charles Handy, 1994)

Young Commonwealth citizens can make a difference in their own community, which will act as a model and an inspiration to others across the world.

Film: Challenging

Deepak Chauhan is 22 now, and was brought up in a small village called Tikawli, in Haryana, India. When he left school, he started farming his ancestral land.

'Farming was great fun in the beginning and I did it with great enthusiasm, but I never intended to take it as my profession. My cousin ran a photography studio in the neighbouring city of Faridabad. Not knowing my way further in life, I went to him. The very feel of the camera in my hands would delight me. I fell in love with this art and wanted to pursue it more seriously.'

Back in Tikawli, a new centre had opened, run by the Jiva Institute and Media Lab Asia. They were looking for young people to train in film-making. What an opportunity for Deepak! He wrote and filmed a video telling the story of Kanya, who was not sent to school because she was a girl. In his community, as a result of this, amazing changes are taking place. Some families are sending their daughters to school.

In many cultures, children who are born with any sort of disability are excluded from society and may even be feared because they seem to be different from everyone else. Some people believe that a disability is a punishment from the devil.

For many years, at Dzorwulu Special School in Ghana the children have been given responsibility to look after African snails. These are a delicacy in Ghana and fetch quite a good price. The money raised goes directly back into school vocational training projects, which not only give the children a chance to learn skills, but go a long way towards counteracting the prejudice they may face in their community. Some of the children learn polishing, and in a country where there is a lot of beautiful woodcarving, this is a skill that is valued.

Dzorwulu School has formed a link with a similar school in England, Durants School, Enfield. They learn from each other and teachers have been on reciprocal visits. The English children have developed a great appreciation of Ghanaian culture, and have their own drumming club (above left).

Chiedu, a Year 11 boy from Nigeria, is a pupil who has really responded to the club. He joins in regularly, and he is aware there is a link between his school and the school in Ghana. In fact, his self-esteem has risen dramatically seeing other black African children on video. He has a natural aptitude for drumming and he is aware of this. It gives him freedom of expression and he expresses himself very spontaneously and seemingly without inhibition.

Breeding African snails and harmony in the community

itudes and causing positive change

'Women in the village too will get an opportunity to give their bit to society, and this is something which is simply not possible without education. Women in my community are getting employed. They are working as computer operators, they stitch, and one has joined the police. They are getting independent. Not only is their self-worth but also their worth for society as a whole being appreciated.'

Deepak's next story showed the dilemma of a young boy whose father died, so he became responsible for providing for his family by farming, yet he desperately wanted to continue his education too. The film showed that, with determination and hard work, it was possible to do both.

'Today I have a secure job as a cameraman and I dream big. I am not stopping at this. I want to further my skills in this direction, and further improve the conditions of my village, my country, my environment.'

Giving a voice to children affected by war

Ulric Quee from Sierra Leone was only nine when he was recruited, by force, as a child soldier.

'When my village was attacked by rebels, I lost my dad and mom and I was the only one left. What should I do and where must I go? I know nothing and I cried all night alone in this very dense forest. I was drinking at a stream then I was surrounded by tall huge men and the one yelled at me: "What are you doing here you small boy? You're a spy and I'm going to kill you now." With these words I started trembling and then he said: "Are you going to join us or choose to die?" Then I say: "Whatever you want to do with me I'm willing."

Ulric became a soldier. He was given an AK 47 rifle and injected with cocaine to make him obedient and capable of killing.

Since he has escaped from his life as a soldier, still only a child, Ulric has been trained in ICT skills thanks to an organisation called iEARN whose mission statement is 'Connecting Youth ... Making a Difference'. It provides Internet access for young people for whom this has been difficult in the past, linking teachers and students in 100 countries worldwide. It alerts many people to issues that have been hidden before.

Ulric finishes by saying: 'My life in the jungle was very fierce. I was doing this, but it was not me that was doing all these things, but the drugs that were in me.'

Building bridges in a divided community

Belfast is a city in Northern Ireland that has had a long history of violence between extremists from the Catholic and Protestant communities.

The Lagan Challenge is a project designed to encourage young people from all over Belfast to be involved in the rejuvenation of both the River Lagan and the inner city, and at the same time, make friendly links with other communities, so often divided by hate and mistrust. Active citizenship stimulates a real sense of pride in the city and the River Lagan is used as an exciting venue for recreation and social events.

'Sometimes the smallest changes to our lives can make the biggest impact on our future.'

This was certainly true for Charlene, a young 14-year-old Protestant girl from West Belfast's Shankill Road, where there has been a long history of high unemployment, civil conflict and little or no hope of a peaceful future. Her community is surrounded by peace walls and man-made barriers, preventing her, and many others like her, from mixing with young Catholics from across the divide, with their different political aspirations and culture. There exists, here, a genuine sense of fear and mistrust.

It is in this background that Charlene grew up, spending most of her life playing in her own area, not being able to venture out of her community for fear of being attacked.

During the summer of 1998, Charlene joined the Lagan Challenge. She was keen to meet young people from the Catholic community and curious about how they lived and played together. For the first time in her life, she was presented with the opportunity to mix freely with young Catholics in a friendly and peaceful environment.

Each week Charlene participated in a number of local history and group work sessions, exploring a shared

past and the common bond of citizenship, fears and aspirations that the young people had for the future. These provided an excellent platform for everyone to build trust and confidence in one another. In no time at all they began to exchange their mobile phone numbers and would meet with each other in the city centre. Some of the young people would even travel out of the safety and security of their own areas to their friends' homes across the divide.

The effect on Charlene was profound, and this is how she describes it: 'I've learnt how to be tolerant, to have respect for other young people of a different religion and tradition, and that stereotypical perceptions are misleading and harmful.'

Charlene's commitment, enthusiasm and willingness to help others paved the way for her to become the first project member to successfully complete training in junior leadership skills. Working closely with the other staff members, she assisted in the supervision of new members, making them feel welcome and encouraging them to participate actively in a number of project sessions, as she herself had been encouraged in the beginning.

As a junior leader, Charlene has helped bring out the best in the young people she now works with and in doing so, has brought out the best in herself, increasing her confidence and self-esteem. Charlene's new ambition in life is to be a professional youth worker and she has just completed training in childcare and child protection.

She tells us: 'I have a real passion to encourage young people here in Belfast to learn to work together for peace. I know that peace won't come tomorrow, or the next day, and I do know that being an active citizen, contributing to the solutions that resolve conflict, will one day bring normality and eventually peace in Northern Ireland.'

Many, many young people across the Commonwealth are very aware of and concerned about the future and the fate of the world. They are, indeed, informed, active and committed Commonwealth citizens.

We should 'never doubt that a small group of committed citizens can change the world, for, indeed, it is the only thing that ever has'. (Margaret Mead, Friends of the Earth, 1992)

chapter 10

how does the Commonwealth work?

Unlike other international organisations, there is no set of rules, treaty or constitution which binds the members of the Commonwealth together. Instead member countries make a commitment to the core values and principles of the Commonwealth as set out in the Singapore and Harare Declarations; and accept Commonwealth practices, such as the use of the English language. The emphasis is always on informality and flexibility.

The Queen on a walkabout

The Queen as Head of the Commonwealth

Before India's decision to become a republic, all the member countries of the Commonwealth recognised the British king or queen as their head of state. India, however, wanted to be a republic not a monarchy. The London Declaration of 1949 said that the British monarch would be a symbol of the free association of independent countries, and as such the Head of the Commonwealth. These words meant that republics could be members since they only accepted the monarch as Head of the Commonwealth not as their own Head of State. Today, most member countries are republics.

Thus when Elizabeth II came to the throne in 1952 she became Head of the Commonwealth. She is a symbol of the association – she has no powers to decide what the Commonwealth should do or how it should conduct its affairs.

However, the Queen has had a very important role in shaping the modern Commonwealth. When she became Queen, she was a young woman. She sympathised with the young African politicians who were campaigning for independence from British rule. Throughout the last 50 years the Queen has shown a great commitment to the Commonwealth, visiting many Commonwealth countries and attending most Heads of Government Meetings.

Sir Shridath Ramphal, who was Commonwealth Secretary-General from 1975 to 1990, spoke of the Queen's attitude to the apartheid regime in South Africa:

'The Queen, as Head of the Commonwealth, stood unambiguously on the side of freedom and justice and democracy in South Africa and unflinchingly for the integrity of the Commonwealth itself.'

Sir Peter Marshall, Chairperson of the Joint Commonwealth Societies' Council, said on the occasion of the Queen's Golden Jubilee:

'Her Majesty's knowledge of the Commonwealth is unrivalled: it is the product not only of wisdom and duty, but also of those yet more basic ingredients of the successful management of public affairs – hard work and goodwill.'

During a Golden Jubilee banquet given in the Queen's honour at the 2002 CHOGM (see below), she said:

'…it is because so many people from every walk of life value this extraordinary community of ours that the Commonwealth has such a deep meaning for me … [The Commonwealth] brings people together and enriches lives. As long as we never lose sight of that goal, I am as sure of the future as I am proud of the past of this great organisation which it has been my privilege to serve since 1952.'

When the Queen dies or if she abdicates, her heir will not automatically become Head of the Commonwealth. It will be up to the Commonwealth heads of government to decide what they want to do about this symbolic role.

Commonwealth Heads of Government Meetings

After the Commonwealth Games, the Heads of Government Meetings (CHOGMs) are the most well known events of the Commonwealth. In the spotlight of the world's media (above), the Commonwealth leaders gather to discuss matters of common interest. The journalists are quick to emphasise disagreements, but the real work of the meetings goes on behind the scenes and away from the press.

Where do they meet?

Before 1971, these meetings were always in London. Since then they have been held every two years in a different Commonwealth country.

1971	**Singapore**
1973	**Ottawa** (Canada)
1975	**Kingston** (Jamaica)
1977	**London** (UK)
1979	**Lusaka** (Zambia)
1981	**Melbourne** (Australia)
1983	**New Delhi** (India)
1985	**Nassau** (The Bahamas)
1987	**Vancouver** (Canada)
1989	**Kuala Lumpur** (Malaysia)
1991	**Harare** (Zimbabwe)
1993	**Limassol** (Cyprus)
1995	**Auckland** (New Zealand)
1997	**Edinburgh** (UK)
1999	**Durban** (South Africa)
2002	**Coolum** (Australia)*
2003	**Abuja** (Nigeria)

*The CHOGM which would normally have taken place in 2001 was postponed until 2002 because of the terrorist attacks in the USA on 11 September 2001.

What happens at CHOGMs?

CHOGMs are big affairs — after all, Commonwealth leaders govern over a quarter of the world's population. These days, heads of government bring large delegations with them — ministers and civil servants. Several hundred people are involved.

The summits open with a formal ceremony, which the Queen usually attends. But thereafter the style of the meeting changes and the informality of the Commonwealth takes over. The leaders of small, developing countries have exactly the same status as those of large, highly developed nations. All sit down together as equals, with a limited number of advisers. Usually, too, the leaders go into 'retreat' — they move to somewhere really quiet, away from the press, and have private discussions.

Over the years, leaders build friendships and are able to talk to each other in a direct and open way, which is unusual in gatherings of world leaders.

At CHOGM 2002: Prime Minister John Howard of Australia (left) with the then President of Kiribati, Teburoro Tito.

Aboriginal dancers at the People's Festival, Brisbane 2001

Consensus-building

One of the remarkable features about Commonwealth summits is that agreement is reached by consensus. No votes are taken – no leader is forced to go along with the wishes of a majority with which he or she may disagree.

The process of consensus-building works like this: On any given topic a group of leaders is likely to have many different opinions. However, there is probably a common core of agreement. For example, the leaders may agree that more girls should go to school; they may disagree about what the Commonwealth should do about it. Through discussions, they try to build and develop the area of agreement – leaders negotiate with each other, conceding a point here, winning a point there. In the end there is consensus – everybody has got part of what they want, no-one has forced their views on others.

What do the leaders talk about?
At CHOGMs, Commonwealth leaders talk about world affairs, such as terrorism. Through consensus, they agree a united Commonwealth view on such matters. But more importantly, they discuss and agree the policies and activities of the Commonwealth for the next two years. It is CHOGM which directs all the activities of the Commonwealth.

At the end of the meeting, the decisions that have been reached and the plans that have been made are made public through a communiqué.

At the end of the 2002 CHOGM the Commonwealth leaders issued a strong condemnation of terrorism. They said:

'We solemnly reaffirm our resolve as a diverse community of nations individually and collectively to take concerted and resolute action to eradicate terrorism'.

What else happens at the CHOGMs?

In recent years, CHOGM has been the focal point around which other gatherings take place. In 2001, in Australia, for example:

- Large numbers of young people gathered in a Commonwealth youth forum. In 2001, the major topics of this forum were youth leadership; development of enterprises; the role of young people; youth participation in democracy; and youth perspectives on international issues. The resolutions of the forum were passed to the Heads of Government.

- There was a meeting of over 500 Commonwealth business leaders.

- There was a meeting of the Commonwealth Local Government Forum.

- The Commonwealth Parliamentary Association's annual conference took place.

- The unofficial Commonwealth family of NGOs and professional associations gathered at the People's Centre where there were exhibitions, and discussions on such matters as democracy, human rights, sustainable development, employment and health. The accompanying People's Festival provided a week of cultural performances, given by 50 groups of artists coming from all over the Commonwealth – there were dancers, drummers, singers and theatrical groups.

The Commonwealth Secretariat

When CHOGM is over, the leaders and their delegations fly home, the forums come to an end, and the journalists go on to cover the next story. The Commonwealth drops out of the headlines, yet it is then that the real work begins. It is the Commonwealth Secretariat's job to carry out the plans and decisions of CHOGM – it is the Secretariat which makes the Commonwealth work.

The mission statement of the Secretariat is:

'We work as a trusted partner for all Commonwealth peoples as a force for peace, democracy, equality and good governance; as a catalyst for global consensus-building; and as a source of assistance for sustainable development and poverty eradication'.

Established in 1965, the Commonwealth Secretariat is based in Marlborough House, London. It was intended to be 'a visible symbol of the spirit of co-operation which animates the Commonwealth'.

Who works at the Secretariat?

There are about 290 people working in the Secretariat. They come from over 35 different Commonwealth countries. Some are seconded by their home governments.

The top job in the Commonwealth is that of the Secretary-General. He or she is elected by CHOGM.

The first two Secretaries-General were Arnold Smith of Canada (1965-75) and Shridath (Sonny) Ramphal of Guyana (1975-90). They guided the Commonwealth through the difficult years of establishing the Secretariat and the association's reputation in the international arena.

From 1990 until 2000 the Secretary-General was Chief Emeka Anyaoku of Nigeria (above). When asked about the most satisfying part of his work he replied:

'[It has] been the new vigour, the new sense of importance and relevance which Commonwealth leaders and Commonwealth peoples throughout have begun to assign to the Commonwealth. It is now widely recognised as a force for democracy and respect for human rights – the basic fundamental values of the Commonwealth'.

In 1999 Don McKinnon of New Zealand (above) was elected by CHOGM to become the new Secretary-General the following year. In his 2001 report he said: 'Which other association enables the Heads of Government of Barbados, Lesotho or Tuvalu to sit down at a table as sovereign equals and share their concerns with the leaders of Canada, India, South Africa or the United Kingdom? ... Accommodating diverse views and customs is ingrained in the ethos of the modern Commonwealth. It has strengthened commitment to consensus and consensus-building, that is, to seeking agreement rather than avoiding it ... It has acted as a bridge builder not only between rich and poor, but also between different interest groups and organisations, on major issues. And always, it has equality, justice and the interests of common people at heart'.

He and two Deputy Secretaries-General oversee the eleven divisions and three specialised units which make up the Secretariat.

The structure of the Commonwealth Secretariat

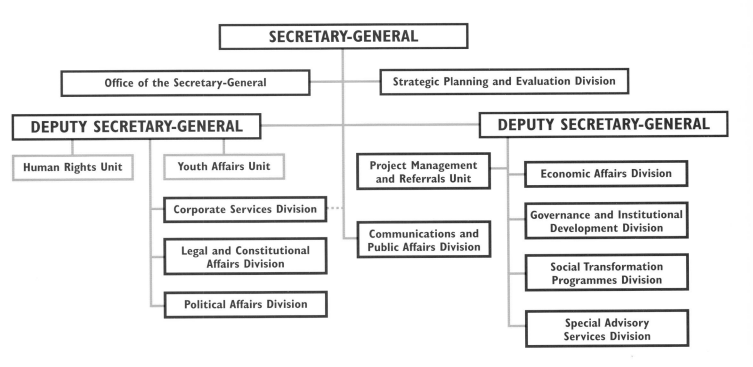

What does the Secretariat do?

Arranges meetings

It is the Secretariat staff that arranges CHOGMs and other meetings of Commonwealth ministers. Ministers of Education, Finance, Health, Law, Women's Affairs and Youth Affairs meet regularly. The Ministers for Youth Affairs, for example, meet every three years – and young people always play an active part in their meetings.

Carries out programmes

It is CHOGM that decides on the priority areas of action for the Commonwealth. The Secretariat converts them into programmes, which all the divisions co-operate in carrying out.
For 2002-2004 the programmes are concerned with:
- democracy and human rights
- good governance and the rule of law
- gender and youth
- poverty reduction and sustainable development
- vulnerability of small states

There are three specialised funds for which activities are managed by the Secretariat:
- CYP: Commonwealth Youth Programme (see page 80)
- CFTC: Commonwealth Fund for Technical Co-operation (see page 64)
- CSC: Commonwealth Science Council

Thirty-six Commonwealth countries belong to the Science Council. This organisation is concerned with, among other things, bridging the 'digital divide' – this is the gap between the countries which have the resources to embrace the new information technology and those that do not. The CSC also supports projects which show how people can use science and technology to improve their lives.

Provides information

The Secretariat is the main source of information about the Commonwealth.

Who pays for it?

For the main work of the Secretariat, each member government provides some money. The amount each pays depends on the size of its population and its level of income. Voluntary payments from member countries pay for the CFTC and CYP.

Other official Commonwealth organisations

Besides the Commonwealth Secretariat, there are two other official organisations in the Commonwealth. These receive funds from the governments of member countries. These are the Commonwealth Foundation, and the Commonwealth of Learning.

The Commonwealth Foundation

This was established in 1966. Its staff also uses Marlborough House but the organisation is much smaller than the Secretariat. The purpose of the Foundation is to strengthen and work with the network of professional associations, non-governmental organisations (NGOs) and civil society groups which make up the People's Commonwealth (see below).

An NGO is a voluntary organisation which is independent of any government or business, and which is not run for profit. Since 1991, the Commonwealth Foundation has organised a forum of Commonwealth non-governmental organisations every four years. It has also ensured that NGOs are represented at Commonwealth Ministers Meetings, such as Health or Youth Affairs.

In Australia in 2001 the Foundation helped to organise a People's Festival which celebrated the diversity of the Commonwealth through exhibitions and cultural events. To encourage cultural activities in the Commonwealth, the Foundation offers prizes for fiction and poetry, short stories and photography, and arts and crafts (see page 74).

The Commonwealth of Learning

Based in Vancouver, this organisation was established in 1988. Its focus is on distance and open learning. (For more information see pages 72-3.)

The People's Commonwealth

In the early days of the modern Commonwealth, most people-to-people contact was through professional associations, for example Commonwealth associations for doctors, nurses, lawyers, etc. In the 1980s there was a burst of activity and a host of new NGOs were formed – their emphasis was more on working with people to improve their lives.

This diagram gives you some idea of the different types of organisations which are in the People's Commonwealth network:

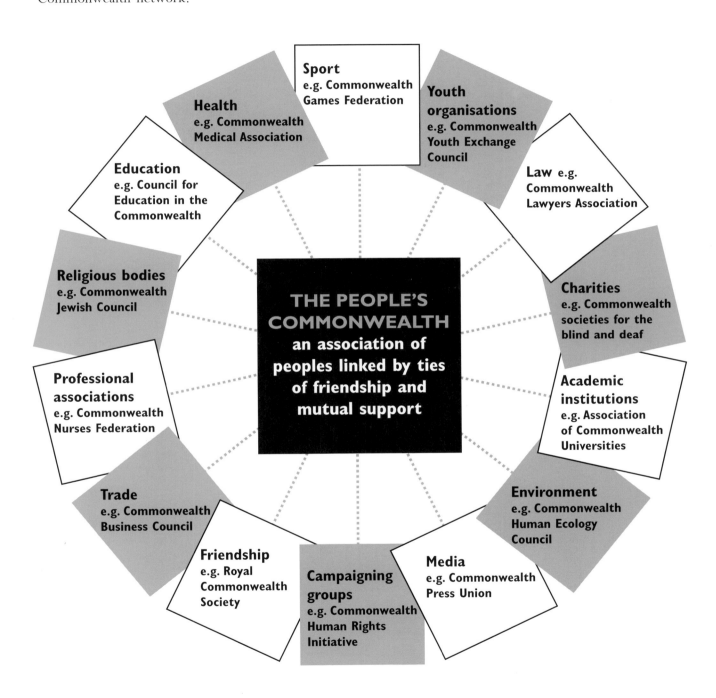

(Adapted from W. David McIntyre, *A Guide to the Contemporary Commonwealth*, page 164)

Every day, within these Commonwealth
organisations, individuals are busy exchanging
information with partners in other countries,
are co-operating with each other and are visiting
each other, to further their common aims.
This vast network of co-operation underpins
the official Commonwealth — it is what makes
the association a 'family'.

chapter 11

the role of the Commonwealth

How many times have we heard someone say:

'We're all in this together'?

In a way, that is how the Commonwealth looks at itself as a grouping of far-flung countries from around the globe. We know this because their representatives — heads of government, cabinet ministers, government officials, members of non-governmental organisations — meet frequently. They discuss their problems, their common interests and how they fit in with the rest of the world. They make decisions on action in their common interests.

It has been many years since the Commonwealth defined itself merely in terms of its past history and colonial ties. It now sees itself, as Commonwealth Secretary-General Don McKinnon says, 'as a global forum for sharing ideas, exchanging knowledge and establishing a cultural dialogue among equal partners'. Its members pool their experience and skills to help each other. At the same time, they continue to uphold the highest ideals of the grouping — belief in equality, justice, democracy and the right of the individual to live freely and in dignity.

Nowadays, more people than ever before travel and conduct business all over the world. Look at the shelves in your nearest supermarket or shop. You may find vegetables from Africa, fruit from the Caribbean, tins of food from Europe, electronic goods from Asia, meat from the Pacific. If you read the newspapers or watch television, you will note how a hurricane in one part of the world can stimulate aid action from another continent, and also affect financial markets, food supplies,

sometimes even politics, elsewhere.

This is what is now called 'globalisation'. It means that all countries are connected in some way and thus interdependent. This is why it is best for major decisions that affect all countries to be agreed by all. That will avoid conflict and the possibility that some countries, usually the smaller and poorer ones, could be unfairly treated and become worse off. The more we are connected with each other, the less we can afford to ignore each other's needs and interests.

The Commonwealth tradition of meeting frequently to agree on problems and action fits in well with this. What is called consensus — agreement by all — has been the hallmark of Commonwealth decision-making for decades. It takes these decisions into other international forums — to the United Nations, the World Bank and regional groupings such as those for Europe and Southern Africa — where similar problems are being discussed, and seeks agreement for the common good there.

By consensus, too, Commonwealth leaders, between 1999 and 2002, agreed on a role for the grouping in this globalised world — one that will match its strengths with needs. The Commonwealth's work for the 21st century will therefore concentrate on the following major areas:

Democracy and rule of law

This is a key building block for stability and development. It promotes:

- individual rights, and thus frees the potential of the individual
- elected government — the right to choose representatives
- respect for the law, both national and international
- conflict prevention and resolution — where the Commonwealth can use its links to head off conflict or to find an agreeable solution for it

Having their say ... eager voters turn up early to vote

Trade and investment opportunities, private sector development

People now talk of countries trading their way out of poverty. It is one of the best ways of ensuring that countries do not have to rely on overseas aid. It gives a country dignity to be more self-reliant and play a valued role in the global economy. The Commonwealth will promote:

- better access to international markets for goods and produce especially from smaller and poorer countries
- business and investment opportunities which will strengthen a country's economy, by providing capital as well as increasing jobs and wages
- the development of the private sector which will stimulate individual enterprise
- information and communications technology so as to bridge the digital divide between rich and poor by bringing better information more quickly to decision-makers and to business

Youth for the future

Two-thirds of the Commonwealth's total population are under 29 years of age and leaders recognise that the future lies in their hands. The Commonwealth will:

- accelerate transfer of skills and knowledge through schemes for youth enterprise, volunteering, mentoring and leadership education
- harness the skills and enthusiasm of young people to contribute to the work of the Commonwealth as a whole

Taking part in the decision making process

In looking to the future, Commonwealth leaders said in 2002:

'We envisage a modern and vibrant Commonwealth working to serve its peoples ... We want the Commonwealth to be an effective defender of democratic freedoms and a peacemaker in conflict, and to work tirelessly in promoting people-centred economic development'.

Schemes for enterprise will promote businesses for young people that will reduce poverty among them. Volunteering will result in transfers of new technologies and new approaches for youth development. Mentoring will link experienced executives and skilled youth volunteers to transfer business planning and practical skills.

In addition to political and economic development, and nurturing the next generation, the Commonwealth continues to support work to improve education, health and equal development of women and men. It does so in partnership not just with member governments, but also with a broad range of non-governmental organisations and other international organisations.

useful addresses and websites

Association of Commonwealth Universities (ACU)
John Foster House
36 Gordon Square
London
WC1H 0PF
UNITED KINGDOM
0044 [0] 20 7380 6700
0044 [0] 20 7387 2655
Email: info@acu.ac.uk
www.acu.ac.uk

British Empire and Commonwealth Museum
Clock Tower Yard
Temple Meads
Bristol
BS1 6QH
UNITED KINGDOM
0044 [0] 117 925 4980
0044 [0] 117 925 4983
Email: staff@empiremuseum.co.uk
www.empiremuseum.co.uk

CAB International (CABI)
Nosworthy Way
Wallingford
Oxon
OX10 8DF
UNITED KINGDOM
0044 [0] 1491 832111
0044 [0] 1491 833508
Email: corporate@cabi.org
www.cabi.org

Commonwealth Association for Corporate Governance (CACG)
Box 34, Havelock
Marlborough
NEW ZEALAND
64 3 574 2502
64 3 574 2519
Email: g.bowes@xtra.co.nz

Commonwealth Association for Mental handicap & Developmental disabilities (CAMHADD)
36A Osberton Place
Sheffield
S11 8XL
UNITED KINGDOM
0044 [0] 114 268 2695
0044 [0] 114 268 2695

Commonwealth Association of Museums
PO Box 30192
Chinook Postal Outlet
Calgary
Alberta
T2H 2V9
CANADA
001 403 938 3190
001 403 938 3190
Email: irvinel@fclc.com

Commonwealth Association for Public administration and Management (CAPAM)
1075 Bay street
Suite 402
Toronto
Ontario
M5S 2B1
CANADA
001 416 920 3337
001 416 920 6574
Email: capam@capam.ca
www.capam.comnet.mt

Commonwealth Association of Science, Technology and Mathematics Education (CASTME)
c/o Education Department,
Commonwealth Secretariat
Malborough House, Pall Mall
London
SW1Y 5HX
UNITED KINGDOM
0044 [0] 20 7747 6282
0044 [0] 20 7747 6287
Email: v.goel@commonwealth.int

Commonwealth Broadcasting Association (CBA)
17 Fleet Street
London
EC4Y 1AA
UNITED KINGDOM
0044 [0] 20 7583 5550
0044 [0] 20 7583 5549
Email: cba@cba.org.uk
www.cba.org.uk

Commonwealth Business Council
18 Pall Mall
London
SW1Y 5JH
UNITED KINGDOM
0044 [0] 20 7930 4920
0044 [0] 20 7930 3944/3945
Email: info@cbcnet.org
www.cbcnet.org

Commonwealth Forestry Association (CFA)
Oxford Forestry Institute
South Parks Road
Oxford
OX1 3RB
UNITED KINGDOM
0044 [0] 1865 271037
0044 [0] 1865 275074
Email: cfa@plants.ox.ac.uk,
cfa_oxford@hotmail.com

Commonwealth Foundation
Marlborough House
Pall Mall
London
SW1Y 5HX
UNITED KINGDOM
0044 [0] 20 7930 3783
0044 [0] 20 7839 8157/7930 3785
Email: geninfo@commonwealth.int
www.commonwealthfoundation.com

Commonwealth of Learning (COL)
1285 West Broadway, Suite 600
Vancouver
BC
V6H 3X8
CANADA
001 604 775 8200
001 604 775 8210
Email: info@col.org
www.col.org

Commonwealth Local Government Forum (CGLF)
59 Southwark Street
London
SE1 0AL
UNITED KINGDOM
0044 [0] 20 7934 9690/9698
0044 [0] 20 7934 9699
Email: info@clgf.org.uk
www.clgf.org.uk

Commonwealth Parliamentary Association (CPA)
Suite 700, Westminster House
7 Millbank
London
SW1P 3JA
UNITED KINGDOM
0044 [0] 20 7799 1460
0044 [0] 20 7222 6073
Email: hq.sec@cpahq.org
www.cpahq.org

Commonwealth Policy Studies Unit (CPSU)
28 Russell Square
London
WC1B 5DS
UNITED KINGDOM
0044 [0] 208 744 1233
0044 [0] 207 862 8820
Email: rbourne@sas.ac.uk
www.cpsu.org.uk

Commonwealth Press Union (CPU)
17 Fleet Street
London
EC4Y 1AA
UNITED KINGDOM
0044 [0] 20 7583 7733
0044 [0] 20 7583 6868
Email: cpu@cpu.org.uk
www.cpu.org.uk

Commonwealth Secretariat
Marlborough House
Pall Mall
London
SW1Y 5HX
UNITED KINGDOM
0044 [0] 20 7747 6500
0044 [0] 20 7930 0827
Email: info@commonwealth.int
(general enquiries)
www.thecommonwealth.org &
www.youngcommonwealth.org

Commonwealth Service Abroad Proramme (CSAP)
Commonwealth Secretariat
Marllborough House, Pall Mall
London
SW1Y 5HX
ENGLAND
0044 [0] 20 7747 6355
0044 [0] 20 7747 6515
Email: p.sardana@commonwealth.int

Commonwealth Telecommunications Organisation (CTO)
Clareville House
26-27 Oxendon Street
London
SW1Y 4EL
UNITED KINGDOM
0044 [0] 20 7930 5516
0044 [0] 20 7930 4248
Email: info@cto.int
www.cto.int

Commonwealth Youth Exchange Council (CYEC)
7 Lion Yard
Tremadoc Road
London
SW4 7NF
UNITED KINGDOM
0044 [0] 20 7498 6151
0044 [0] 20 7720 5403
Email@cyec.demon.co.uk
www.cyec.org.uk

Commonwealth Youth Programme (CYP)
Commonwealth Secretariat
Marlborough House, Pall Mall
London
SW1Y 5HX
ENGLAND
0044 [0] 20 7747 6462/3
0044 [0] 20 7747 6549
Email: cyp@commonwealth.int
www.cypyough.org

Disabled Peoples Intermnational Commonwealth Committee
Global Project Office Room 109
11 Belgrave Road
London
SW1V 1RB
UNITED KINGDOM
0044 [0] 20 7834 0477
0044 [0] 20 7821 9539
Email: admin@daa.org.uk
www.dpi.org

Institute of Commonwealth Studies
27-28 Russell Square
London
WC1B 5DS
UNITED KINGDOM
0044 [0] 20 7862 8844
0044 [0] 20 7255 2160
Email: ics@sas.ac.uk
www.sas.ac.uk/commonwealthstudies

Royal Agricultural Society of the Commonwealth (RASC)
2 Grosvenor Gardens
London
SW1W 0DH
UNITED KINGDOM
0044 [0] 259 9678
0044 [0] 259 9675
Email: rasc@commagshow.org
www.commagshow.org

The Royal Commonwealth Society (RCS)
18 Northumberland Avenue
London
WC2N 5BJ
UNITED KINGDOM
0044 [0] 20 7930 6733
0044 [0] 20 7930 9705
Email: info@rcsint.org
www.rcsint.org

Sight Savers International (The Royal Commonwealth Society for the Blind)
Grosvenor Hall
Bolnore Road
Haywards Heath
West Sussex
RH16 4BX
UNITED KINGDOM
0044 [0] 1444 446 600
0044 [0] 1444 446 688
Email:
generalinormation@sightsavers.org
www.sightsavers.org

index